The MYTHS SCIENCE *of*

EDITOR | KIRSTEN BIRKETT

A
kategoria
BOOK

GW00715489

❦ **MATTHIAS MEDIA**

The Myths of Science
© Matthias Media, 2003

Matthias Media
(St Matthias Press Ltd. ACN 067 558 365)
PO Box 225
Kingsford NSW 2032 Australia
Telephone: (02) 9663 1478; Facsimile: (02) 9663 3265
International: +61-2-9663 1478; Facsimile: +61-2-9663 3265
Email: info@matthiasmedia.com.au
Internet: www.matthiasmedia.com.au

Distributed in the United Kingdom by:
The Good Book Company
Telephone: 0845-225-0880
Facsimile: 9845-225-0990
Email: admin@thegoodbook.co.uk
Internet: www.thegoodbook.co.uk

Distributed in South Africa by:
Christian Book Discounters
Telephone: (021) 685 3663
Email: peter@christianbooks.co.za

Unless otherwise indicated, all Scripture quotations are from the HOLY BIBLE, NEW INTERNATIONAL VERSION. Copyright © 1973, 1978, 1984 International Bible Society. Used by permission of Zondervan Bible Publishers.

ISBN 1 876326 57 3

Cover design and typesetting by Joy Lankshear Design Pty Ltd.

Acknowledgments

'Galileo: history v. polemic', by Kirsten Birkett,
first appeared in *kategoria*, 1996, 1, pp. 13-42.

✝

'Miracles and rational belief', by Roger White,
first appeared in *kategoria*, 1997, 5, pp. 9-26.

✝

'Addendum: miracles as evidence for Christianity', by
Archie Poulos, first appeared in *kategoria*, 1997, 5, pp. 29-32.

✝

'Giordano Bruno: enigmatic martyr', by Kirsten Birkett,
first appeared in *kategoria*, 1997, 6, pp. 27-43.

✝

'Darwin and the fundamentalists', by Kirsten Birkett,
first appeared in *kategoria*, 1996, 2, pp. 25-53.

✝

'History gone wrong', review of *Summer for the Gods: The Scopes
Trial and America's Continuing Debate over Science and Religion*,
Edward J. Larson, reviewed by Kirsten Birkett,
first appeared in *kategoria*, 1998, 11, pp. 47-58.

Table of Contents

About the Contributors

KIRSTEN BIRKETT
Kirsten Birkett (B.Sc. Hons, Ph.D., UNSW) is the editor of the quarterly journal *kategoria* and author of several books including two on the interaction between Christianity and science.

ARCHIE POULOS
Archie Poulos (B.E., UNSW; B.Th., Dip.A., M.A., Moore Theological College) is the Training Coordinator at the Ministry Training Strategy and attends the Cross-Culture Bible Church in Arncliffe, Sydney.

ROGER WHITE
Roger White (B.A. Hons, UNSW; Ph.D., MIT) is Assistant Professor of Philosophy at New York University specializing in philosophy of science, epistemology and metaphysics.

Preface

WHEN CHRISTIANITY IS mentioned in the context of science or modern knowledge, a few old pennies will inevitably turn up. First, we'll be reminded that although the church tried to suppress his findings, Galileo still managed to prove that the earth was not the centre of the universe, as Christianity had taught. Then we'll be told that David Hume showed that miracles could not have happened, and that Darwin built on this scientific understanding by proving that life was not the special creation and plan of God, but a natural process. Any lingering inclination towards God can be banished by remembering the times when Christianity has brutally, but ultimately unsuccessfully, opposed the forward march of enlightenment; when, for instance, Giordano Bruno was martyred for his beliefs about astronomy, or when the Scopes Trial saw the blind irrationalism of Fundamentalists pitted against evolution.

None of these stories is true. Some have the gist of the conflict right but entirely misread the conclusion; others simply have the facts of the matter wrong. As common mythology, they drift around the academic and popular media, to be mentioned when it suits the commentator but rarely if ever to be actually examined. These myths have frequently been cited by intelligent thinkers who really should know better; in my own hearing, Stephen Jay Gould and Bishop John Selby Spong have both been perpetrators. It is not surprising, then, that these myths are accepted as plain historical fact in more general discourse—in newspapers, school texts or television programmes.

kategoria is a journal which, from its first issue, took on such challenges, to put on record in a clear, accessible and well-referenced manner what the historical accounts actually say. As part of its general aim to provide a Christian critique of our contemporary intellectual world, *kategoria* has also periodically taken up popular distortions of fact which are used as arguments against Christianity, and put them under the spotlight. We are pleased to have been able to do that; but journals date, and are left on the shelf and forgotten. This present volume aims to bring some of these issues back into the spotlight, to remind ourselves and others that these myths are still circulating, are still wrong, and still need to be challenged.

We hope in future to bring together other *kategoria* collections, so that topics or themes that have been examined over a number of journal issues can be available in a single book. This not only makes it easier for the reader to find the articles on that particular theme, but continues to bring before the public the necessary challenges and corrections to a non-Christian world view. We hope you enjoy them.

1.
Galileo: history v. polemic
Kirsten Birkett

In 1616, a board of theologians for the Roman Catholic Church discussed the new Copernican theory. The result of that deliberation was an official decree stating that to say the sun is at the centre of the world and immovable is 'foolish and absurd' and 'formally heretical'; and to say that the Earth moves is similarly foolish and 'erroneous in the faith'.

Sixteen years later Galileo Galilei faced the Inquisition on charges of heresy because of his belief in that same theory. He was ordered to abjure his heretical opinions—that is, to state that he firmly believed that the Earth did not move—and was sentenced to a prison term with penance.

Galileo, the symbol of free thought and the power of science, was brutally crushed by the blind stupidity which is the inevitable consequence of an institution based on revelation rather than discovery. It was a classic and poignant example of the irreconcilable clash between the two worlds. Galileo, threatened with torture and the might of the Catholic Church, recanted and stated through clenched teeth that he did not believe that which he knew to be true. Yet the spirit of free thought could not be suppressed. As he left the room with its instruments of torture, he muttered, "...and yet it turns".

It is a picture that suits propagandists of many types, but unfortunately it lacks a certain element—it is not true. Though non-historians may find this surprising, it is not a recent or innovative claim. For decades, historians of science and early modern Europe have recognised this glib picture as a caricature—yet the caricature refuses to die, held up by those whose propaganda it suits. The 'Galileo incident' as it has come to be known in the literature, can be described as any number of things, but to see it as an example of Church dogmatism *versus* free thought rather misses the point. It was a political battle between warring academics and academic traditions, fought over the issues of disciplinary boundaries and academic prestige; it was a clash between medieval and modern conceptions of knowledge; it was a matter of power politics. It was a time when the educational structure was changing and old-school academics fought hard to maintain their traditional privileges; and when, in a changing society, intellectual prestige was a stake in social hierarchies. Put this against the background of Reformation and counter-Reformation, after the Catholic Church had been shaken to the roots by Protestant demands for the individual's right to personal access to the Bible, and it is not surprising that somewhere along the line, someone was charged with heresy. The fact that it was the Copernican system that precipitated the trial is (for the Catholic Church at least) historically unfortunate. Crises could have occurred over a range of other issues, given different circumstances; and had Galileo been a less abrasive character, had his involvement in academic politics been less prominent, and had the political situation been less volatile, it might not have happened at all.

Galileo's career does not demonstrate an instance of Christianity *versus* science. It *does* demonstrate what happens when old science is challenged by a new theory—many of those in the scientific establishment react with scepticism and dismiss the new challenger. Galileo's story is really about Aristotelianism clashing with modern mathematical science. Galileo fought for a new science, against the entrenched conservatism of an intellectual system which had been accepted for centuries, and against individuals in the universities who were not at all willing to have their jobs and their professional reputations challenged. The main lessons we learn from Galileo are about how science changes. Apart from that, Galileo's career demonstrates how dangerous politics can be—for once Galileo became embroiled in the political scene of the seventeenth-century papal court, he was in a very risky position.

Galileo's enemy was not Christianity. He considered himself a devout Christian, and in any case many Protestant Christians had no problems with his work. Galileo had many enemies, most of them academics, and he played a dangerous political game. This essay is the story of how and why Galileo lost. It does not attempt to duplicate the already detailed original research on Galileo's life and trial. There is certainly no need to do so; the historical facts of the case have been well established for decades. Here is presented a summary of modern research, in an attempt to move behind the veils which have shrouded this fascinating historical story.

Old science meets new innovations

What first becomes obvious in looking at the Galileo events is that the battle was not 'science' against an outside foe, Christian or otherwise, so much as old science against new science.[1] It is a battle which has been repeated again and again throughout history. Newtonian physics seemed definitive until Einstein presented a new theory. Heat was explained as an accumulation of phlogiston until thermodynamics was developed. In retrospect, it is easy to pick the winners, but at the time such debates are usually very confusing. There are always more bad guesses than good ones, so how does one tell if the new theory is actually better than the old? Should scientists merely extract the good bits from the new theory and incorporate them into the old? Should the old be overthrown entirely in favour of the new?

Such a competition was played out in the astronomy of the late sixteenth and early seventeenth centuries. The old theory was geocentrism, in which the Earth was at the centre of the universe, with planets (including the sun and moon) and stars revolving around it. All physics, dynamics and matter theory backed up the cosmology. The new theory was heliocentrism, with the sun at the centre of the universe and the Earth, one of the planets, revolving around it. We, of course, know which theory won. The heroes of the story for twentieth-century viewers are those who supported the heliocentric universe. At the beginning of the seventeenth century, however, the geocentric universe looked far more likely—and it was the scientists of the day who thought so.

✠

In 1543, in the last year of his life, a modest Polish astronomer named Nicholas Copernicus published a speculative astronomical theory. It was in a work entitled *De revolutionibus orbium coelestium*—'The revolution of the heavenly spheres'. It was different from the old Ptolemaic theory, in placing the sun rather than the Earth at the centre of the universe. It was *like* the old theory in that all the planets moved in circles around the centre.

Any theory which postulates circular motion for the planets cannot possibly fit what we see in the sky (the planets actually move in ellipses). In the old Ptolemaic system many adjustments and additions to the circular model had to be made. Theoretically, with enough additions, the model could fit observation exactly—but it was a very clumsy system. Copernicus, by putting the sun at the centre of the system, managed to reduce the number of additional adjustments necessary to make the theory work. Nevertheless, it was still a clumsy system. Copernicus' theory was 'better' from a scientific point of view, in the sense that it was slightly simpler and explained a few astronomical events more satisfactorily, but it was by no means overwhelmingly convincing.[2]

Copernicus' work is important in putting the Galileo debate in context. We speak of 'The Copernican Revolution' as a crucial moment in Western history, when Copernicus discovered after centuries of error that in fact the Earth moves around the sun. Yet it was not quite like that. Copernicus' theory was, from a purely scientific point of view, only marginally better. Of course he was right, but how could people know that at the time? Besides, he was not completely 'right'—his commitment to circular motion meant that his theory necessarily had problems.

This helps to explain the fairly luke-warm reaction to Copernican theory in the years following its publication. The unpopularity of the theory was not due to Church interference, or Christian dogma—the theory was a matter of technical astronomy, and only of real interest to fellow astronomers. On the whole, they were not much impressed. Of those who showed any interest, most merely made use of Copernicus' improved calculating techniques but ignored or rejected the theory as a new way of understanding the universe. In England (for example), the first clear exposition of Copernican theory was not until 1576, in the only work that century which explicitly endorsed the theory. Even those astronomers who were mildly in favour of Copernicanism were inclined to regard it as an adaptation of the Ptolemaic system, and used a semi-Copernican theory in which the Earth rotated in the centre of the universe.[3]

By 1600 only ten astronomers can be identified who thought Copernicus was right.[4] In other words, Copernican theory was not the great overnight revolution. It was a relatively unsuccessful addition to astronomical knowledge, which the majority of professional astronomers failed to take up. The Church decision to reject it in 1616, though in hindsight wrong and made for the wrong reasons, was not at the time so very irrational. Galileo was not defending the forward march of scientific free-thought against reactionary dogmatism; he defended a speculative theory with little corroborating evidence, in opposition to the majority of scholars of the day.

✖

There is a deep and important reason why Copernican theory was not convincing as a new scientific theory. It had no physics to back it up. It is all very well to hypothesise that the Earth moves around the sun—and certain astronomical observations might thereby be better accounted for—but what makes the Earth move? Copernicus had no answers. He had no laws of motion, and no theory of gravity (that was to come two centuries later, when Isaac Newton finally developed his basic laws of physics). At the time, the only known physics was Aristotelian.

According to Aristotle, 'earth'—regarded as an element in itself—does not fall 'down' but is attracted by nature to the centre of the universe. That is why the

Earth is at the centre; it is the place where matter naturally congregates. The heavenly bodies—suns, planets, stars—are of an entirely different kind of matter, whose nature is to move in circles and which is not attracted to the centre of the universe.[5] In such a physics there is no place for a moving Earth. The moving planets were, by definition, *not* earth. Copernicus' theory did not fit into Aristotelian physics, and he did not have a new physics in which to embed a new astronomy. This was a serious lack. It was as if today someone proposed that the moon literally gets bigger and smaller every month—it fits what we see in the sky, but it makes no sense according to what we know about matter and the laws of gravity.

The theory was not worthless, by any means. It had a mathematical elegance that Ptolemaic theory lacked—enough to impress Galileo, who was a very competent mathematician. Without proper physical laws, however, it could not hope to gain widespread acceptance amongst the academic community; in particular, amongst the physicists, or natural philosophers as they were known.

This clash with Aristotelian thought is something we must take seriously. It is hard to imagine now just how immense a challenge Copernican theory was. If it were true, the entire body of received knowledge about physics—laws of motion, theories of matter, the most fundamental ideas about what the universe is made of and why it behaves the way it does—would have to change. When Galileo began championing Copernican theory, he was not merely suggesting an interesting new technical piece of astronomy. He was, implicitly at first and later explicitly, challenging centuries of accepted knowledge.

Aristotle's system of knowledge was remarkably satisfying and complete. He was regarded as having solved essentially all the problems of the physical universe.[6] Aristotle's laws worked, they explained everything, and civilised humanity had recognised that for centuries. If there was to be any differing opinion, it could perhaps come from those who preferred Plato to Aristotle; but that an astronomer could come up with an entirely new theory was ridiculous, and that Galileo would actually defend such a theory and teach it to his students was very worrying. It was quite natural that his fellow academics opposed him. It was, after all, the duty of established scholars to protect the young from dangerous ideas.

It is often quoted as a laughable example of blind dogmatism that some Aristotelian scholars refused to look through Galileo's telescope to see the moons of Jupiter. They insisted that even if they saw something, it must be a trick, and so refused even to look. Yet from a scientific point of view they had a point. They knew, from their knowledge of the established body of physics, that there could be no moons of Jupiter. What is more, Galileo was unable to explain satisfactorily how the telescope worked. Yet he expected the philosophers to overturn centuries of knowledge on the basis of this mysterious metal tube. There was some justification in their refusal to play his games. In their eyes it was Galileo who was ridiculous—even pitiable—for thinking he could teach anything to Aristotle.[7]

✝

Part of the Aristotelian world view was something which twentieth-century readers, particularly those with any scientific education, will find very hard to grasp. That is, *mathematics had no place in physics*. Natural philosophy did *not* use mathematics, because in general, mathematics was not thought of as something which described the real world. Although we take for granted in modern science that mathematics is the foundation of study of the physical world, this is a modern belief. In Galileo's time, it was a totally alien concept to most philosophers that mathematics might model nature. Indeed, it is not an obvious concept at all. Think about it for a minute. Why should a mathematical equation be the same as something that happens in the real world? Is there any reason for that? Even if one equation happens to correspond to physical reality, why should we expect all natural phenomena to have a mathematical basis?

In Galileo's day, nature was not thought of as mathematical. These days when we say we understand a natural phenomena scientifically, we generally mean we know the mathematics that describes it. We understand projectiles because we can describe the parabolic equations involved. In Aristotelian physics, however, to understand something was to know its inner essence, and the end towards which it moved. In broad terms, nature was thought of as teleological, moving towards its purpose, rather than a machine with specifications that can be described mathematically. For Galileo to present *mathematical* arguments for the superiority of his theories was regarded as entirely irrelevant. He was wasting people's time; it was as if he had failed to understand the basic premises of the problem. "[T]he propositions and the proofs of mathematics do not succeed in demonstrating the strength and the true causes of the operations of nature", one Aristotelian put it.[8] Why should mathematics teach anything about physics? There were entirely different disciplines. You may as well study logic to find out about history. This was precisely the point made by one of Galileo's Aristotelian opponents, Vincenzo di Grazia.

> Before we consider Galileo's demonstrations, it seems necessary to prove how far from the truth are those who wish to prove natural facts by means of mathematical reasoning, among whom, if I am not mistaken, is Galileo. All the sciences and all the arts have their own principles and their own causes by means of which they demonstrate the special properties of their own object. It follows that we are not allowed to use the principles of one science to prove the properties of another. Therefore anyone who thinks he can prove natural properties with mathematical arguments is simply demented, for the two sciences are very different.[9]

It is easy to see how difficult it was for such scholars to

accept Galileo's work. For them, not only did Galileo have bizarre theories, but his very means of defending them was unscholarly. Galileo replied vehemently, defending his methodology just as loudly as he defended his theories, but he had no justification which could be convincing. Until modern science was well established, mathematics had nothing to do with physical phenomena.

✝

No debate is ever conducted entirely on the basis of high ideals. That is why, to understand properly the opposition to Galileo we must delve into the murky waters of academic infighting. Galileo was not merely challenging ideas; he was challenging the people who held those ideas, and people in the sixteenth and seventeenth centuries were no less self-interested or status-conscious than they are now. This reality of human nature, though it takes some of the lofty ring out of the story, was probably one of the biggest obstacles to acceptance of Copernican theory. Astronomers in Galileo's day, no matter how clever, did not do physics.

Astronomers in the sixteenth century were regarded as 'mere mathematicians', and that was an insult. As we have seen, mathematics was not thought of as having anything to do with the real world. Consequently, astronomy was not about reality. It was about mathematical calculations. Astronomers created tables and star charts which would enable people to know where the planets were in the sky at any time, and draw up astrological predictions. In his lifetime, Copernicus was best known for his assistance in reforming the calendar. No-one thought that astronomers necessarily knew how the universe really worked. Imagine a computer programme which has dates of previous eclipses fed in, and an algorithm for calculating from that data when future eclipses will be. It can tell you the answer, but it tells you nothing about what is really happening in an eclipse. Astronomers were like that. They came up with answers—but they didn't decide what really happened in the physical universe. That was the domain of the natural philosophers. The disciplinary difference was reflected in position and salary. Astronomers were the lowest of the low in universities. There was no such thing as a doctorate in astronomy in Italian universities—it was only taught at an undergraduate level. In fact, most astronomers also studied medicine in the hope of gaining more money and status.[10] Astronomers were mere calculators—not real intellectuals at all.[11]

Galileo Galilei was one of this group. He was the son of a court musician, and though he studied medicine at his father's wish he never completed his degree. His interest was always mathematics, and he enrolled himself in private lessons outside the regular university curriculum. On his own he worked on physics and hydrostatic problems, and gave private lessons in maths. Amongst other things, he lectured on the geometry of Dante's hell until he obtained his first position as a lecturer in mathematics at the University of Pisa. He later moved to be Professor of Mathematics at the University of Padua. He continued giving private lessons, developing his own ideas based on Archimedes rather than Aristotle. He wrote a treatise on fortifications; invented a horse-driven pump, a military compass, and a thermometer; experimented with the pendulum, observed the supernova of 1604,[12] and developed theories on hydrostatics and projectiles. Yet he remained, overall, a low-status intellectual on a low salary.

Galileo could not but be intensely irritated by this situation. He was a brilliant mathematician, with an international reputation for his observations and inventions. He had what he thought were sound theories about physics, yet he was still not allowed to be thought of, or called, a 'philosopher'. It was more than a title, as he well knew—without it, he was simply not allowed to contribute to discussions about the way the world actually is. He wanted to be taken seriously as a theorist and an intellectual. In other words, he wanted to change, single-handedly, the disciplinary boundaries that had been in place for centuries. It is some testimony to his force of personality and entrepreneurial ability that to a certain extent he succeeded—but at the cost of pushing people very hard, with disastrous consequences for himself.

✳

Galileo created for himself what has been called "a new socio-political identity".[13] In other words, he quit his university job and made a lateral career move. As we have seen, Galileo's battle was with Aristotelian

philosophers who were highly offended that a mathematician would challenge them at all. Normally, this
kind of academic battle would be dealt with internally,
in the academic environment, through debate, publication, and so on. Galileo, however, refused to play on
their terms. He was not going to let a stagnant academic network stifle him. He moved out of the university system to become a court philosopher.

It was a brilliant career move, making political capi-
tal from his scientific work. In 1608, with the use of the
telescope for which was to become famous, Galileo discovered the moons of Jupiter. Though this is most
often cited as the empirical vindication of Copernican
theory (and certainly helped Galileo's arguments for
Copernicanism),[14] at the time the main use Galileo
made of his discovery was political. He dedicated the
moons of Jupiter to Cosimo II, the Medici Grand-
Duke of Florence. In beautiful prose he compared the
moons to the four virtues, inescapably attached to
Jupiter, who was symbolic of Cosimo I, founder of the
hereditary Medici dynasty. Galileo's flattery paid off. In
1610 he was granted a position at the Medici court,
with no teaching duties, at the staggering salary of
1000 scudi per year[15] and with the coveted title of
'philosopher'.[16]

Court life had its drawbacks. Galileo was not
required to teach, but he was expected to perform.
Patrons such as Cosimo II enjoyed participating in
intellectual life through hosting debates on interesting
or controversial topics. The patron gained credit when

his philosopher won debates, especially if the philosopher did so with wit and cleverness as well as profundity. This meant that Galileo was 'on call' to debate opposing positions or answer questions put by other nobles. He could be expected to answer detailed scientific questions with little time for preparation or for considering the wider implications (for instance, theological) of what he said. What is more, the court audience applauded satirical, biting wit—which Galileo was only too happy to provide, as this suited his rather acerbic personality.[17]

This combination of factors meant that Galileo was in a position to be highly offensive to university philosophers. He had deliberately rejected the university system and its status rankings. He had taken the title 'philosopher' even though he was 'only' an astronomer. He was encouraged to bypass the academic subtleties and niceties, instead approaching debates as a chance to score rhetorical points. He was in a position to be offensive, and he lived up to his potential.

Not long after his appointment as court philosopher, Galileo took part in a dispute with various leading Aristotelian philosophers on the nature of floating bodies. It began at an informal meeting of professors and young Florentine gentlemen, at which Galileo put forward his theory of why objects float. His views were, to say the least, in the minority; and it was claimed that Lodovico delle Colombe, who was not present at the time, would prove him wrong. It was a potentially volatile situation. Colombe was an old enemy of

Galileo, a respected Aristotelian who had suffered under Galileo's sarcasm. They exchanged letters with increasing heat. At the same time, Galileo debated the question at court in the customary style before visiting cardinals. One of them, Cardinal Maffeo Barberini, sided with Galileo and was impressed by his wit and learning—an incident which was to have important consequences later.

Nevertheless Galileo's relationship with the Aristotelian establishment was degenerating. Under Cosimo's urging, he moved to official publication in 1612 with his forceful *Discourse on Floating Bodies*. A reply was published under the name 'The Unknown Academician' (actually the overseer of Pisa University), in a surprisingly mild and light-hearted manner considering the provocation Galileo had offered. This was followed by three Aristotelian attacks by Giorgio Coresio (a lecturer in Greek), Lodovico delle Colombe himself, and Vincenzio di Grazia, a professor in philosophy.[18] These were by no means lighthearted; the authors' enmity was becoming quite obvious. It was a debate about physics, but there was much more at stake—Galileo was arguing for his own theories against Aristotle, to the academics who relied on Aristotle for their position, prestige and world view. What's more, Galileo's biting sarcasm thoroughly ridiculed his opponents. He made bitter personal enemies from what should have been a professional dispute.[19]

✝

Galileo was by this time 48 years old, a highly paid and important court personage, and a world-famous astronomer whose telescopes were in demand from nobles all over Europe. He had made bitter enemies in the academic world by treading on disciplinary toes and treating established academics with scorn and personal ridicule—but won the debates, and won respect as a philosopher amongst the court literati. He had taken on the academic establishment and won. Not many Aristotelians had been convinced by his arguments, but they had been unable to silence him. At this stage, he had had no trouble with Church authorities; if anything, they respected him as a talented astronomer.[20] This raises an important question. If the battle was not really 'religion *v.* science' but 'old science *v.* new science', why did the Church get involved at all?

It is probably fair to say that Galileo's enemies, unable to defeat him in logical argument or by social pressure, took the battleground to the Church.[21] Galileo had not allowed his opponents to silence him in the normal ways, so they looked to silence him through creating theological trouble. There is evidence of a deliberate strategy used against Galileo. Certain of Galileo's enemies formed the loosely organised group known as the 'Liga', apparently lead by Lodovico delle Colombe.[22] The group also drew upon disgruntled clerics such as a certain Father Lorini who had received criticism from Galileo in the past, and the young Dominican Friar Tommaso Caccini (who may have simply delighted in stirring up trouble). These men openly accused Galileo of contradicting the Bible, and set about creating popular suspicion against Galileo in order to catch the attention of the Church authorities.

It was an unfair move, and it is possible to speculate that without this deliberate opposition Galileo's trial may never have happened. Theologians had traditionally allowed philosophers space in which to develop ideas; the medieval Church was not Orwell's Big Brother. Philosophical speculation and discussion was the province and lifeblood of the universities, and though the Church secured the boundaries of admissible doctrine it did not normally dictate what could be discussed.[23] The Church was not out to silence Galileo. Indeed, Galileo's telescopic discoveries had been accepted and endorsed by Jesuit astronomers when he travelled to Rome in 1611: he was not without Church support.

The trouble began with one of the impromptu court debates in which the nobility delighted. At a lunchtime banquet, a university professor announced to the Grand-Duchess Christina (mother of Grand-Duke Cosimo II) that the idea of a moving Earth contradicted Scripture. Galileo was not present at the time, but an ex-pupil of his, Castelli, was; and Christina challenged him on the spot to defend Galileo against this charge. Castelli survived the ordeal as best he could, and immediately wrote to Galileo explaining what had happened. Galileo took up the challenge. Perhaps he had little choice; he had been challenged on a very serious matter before the Grand-Duchess, and probably had to respond in self-protection. He wrote back to

Castelli knowing his letter would be circulated, explaining how he thought the Bible should best be interpreted on such matters.

Galileo was not allowed to leave it there. In what appears to be an effort to incite public opinion against him, Thomas Caccini preached publicly against Galileo in Florence. Then Father Lorini managed to get a copy of Galileo's letter to Castelli. He sent it, with a formal complaint, to the Inquisition.

It was not immediately a disaster. The letter itself was judged harmless. Caccini, however, not content with the lack of response to the letter, went to Rome personally and denounced Galileo to the Inquisition. It was time for Galileo to defend himself more publicly. He wrote a long treatise addressed to the Grand-Duchess Christina—a work of theology, explaining how the Bible should be interpreted, quoting from the Church fathers to back up his argument.

✢

It appears he had gone too far. In writing this treatise, Galileo showed what can be characterised (depending on the slant of the writer) as pugnacious arrogance, selfless dedication to truth or political naivety, and was probably a bit of all three.[24] He certainly did not proceed with much humility. He may have been forced into this debate, but he carried it through with the same vigour he had used against the Aristotelians. Whatever the cause, Galileo produced a treatise telling theologians how they ought to do theology. Coming from an astronomer, with no theological training—however important his court position—this was not likely to be well accepted. It also brought him into direct conflict with Cardinal Bellarmine, one of the most influential cardinals in the Inquisition and indeed perhaps in the Church.

Cardinal Bellarmine,[25] a Jesuit, had spent his life fighting Protestantism. He was the professor of Controversial Theology at the Collegio Romano, one of the major universities in Rome. He was a polemicist, not a speculative philosopher, and though he was intellectually quite capable of understanding Galileo's arguments, he was used to making definitive judgements in the 'life and death' battle against heresy. He had also spent his life fighting Protestants who claimed freedom to interpret the Bible as they wished, and so would naturally be very wary of an individual with no Church authority, albeit a loyal Catholic, who wanted to reinterpret Scripture to accomodate his theories.[26]

Bellarmine had lectured in astronomy early in his career. His lectures give some insight into his character and reveal why he could not possibly have agreed with Galileo. Bellarmine considered theology to be far above astronomy. Indeed, in the face of eternity he could not understand why men were so interested in the mere physical structure of this ephemeral universe. He was happy to let astronomers disagree over technical details, and considered it not the place of theologians to be involved in such disputes. This was not a statement in favour of intellectual autonomy for astronomers—on the contrary, it reflects how unimportant he thought astronomy really was. It meant that theologians were free "to select among them the one which best corresponds to the Sacred Scripture".[27]

Bellarmine had already given Galileo an indirect warning before Caccini's attack. A Carmelite Friar, Foscarini, had written a treatise on Copernicanism and very properly sent it to Bellarmine, as an influential scholar, for comment. Bellarmine had answered in a public letter which he clearly intended Galileo to read. He warned Foscarini to be careful; the Copernican theory was just an hypothesis, and no-one should claim that any such theory was physically true, particularly if it required an alternative reading of Scripture. Galileo's letter to Christina can be seen as an answer to this public warning.

It was an ambitious essay. Galileo's treatise challenged Bellarmine on his own ground, which was hardly tactful. Galileo quoted extensively from Augustine as part of his argument, in the confident tone of a professional. Bellarmine, a serious patristic scholar, would have known far more about Augustine's view of Scripture than Galileo, and would hardly have taken kindly to Galileo instructing him in what Augustine said.[28] To make it worse, Galileo could not, or did not, hold back his sarcastic wit. He lampooned theologians as narrow-minded— not a good idea when Bellarmine was one of them.

The matter had become official, and was dealt with quickly. Galileo came to Rome, and the matter of Copernican theory was considered by a panel of theologians (undoubtedly under Bellarmine's influence) for a brief three days. This is hardly long enough to consider a question of such importance, we would think; but the question is of far more importance to us than it would have been to the Church at the time. All that the theologians saw, it seems, was yet another challenge to Church authority by an isolated troublemaker. It would be nipped in the bud. Copernicus' book was condemned, and Galileo was told not to hold or defend the theory. Galileo himself was not officially mentioned in any condemnation, nor was he disciplined, probably due to his powerful court connections.

For the time being, it was over. Although Galileo was not discredited or humiliated, he had been silenced—a victory for his opponents. In the battle of new science against old science, old science had won this skirmish at least. The Aristotelians, who were not convinced about Copernicanism on scientific grounds, and who had failed (due to Galileo's clever tactics) to defeat it in academic circles, had finally seen it come to grief against Church power.

So far, the story has yet to show much of a battle between Christianity and science. The Church was brought into the debate by others; there was no inevitable clash. In the end, Bellarmine, living in an old-world Aristotelian universe, was not about to accept the arguments of the new-world Galileo. Bellarmine saw no reason to change his belief that the Bible taught a stationary earth. At one point, he had asserted that given sufficient proof, he could change his mind about the

Bible; but it was clear that he never considered an astronomer capable of giving proof weighty enough to challenge the Church fathers. (Remember, also, that Galileo did not *have* any proof for his theory.) The arguments were conducted on different terms. It so happened that Bellarmine held the power, so he won.

Papal politics

Old science had achieved its purpose: Galileo was silenced. There was no need for a further trial. Why was it, then, that sixteen years later Galileo would personally appear before the Inquisition, facing charges of heresy?

In this second stage of his famous career, the conflict moved away from old science defending itself against new science. That battle was at least (more or less) clearly defined. Galileo's final downfall and condemnation, on the other hand, was the result of a very messy political situation in which Galileo believed the wrong promises, pushed the wrong people too hard and made the wrong enemies. It was not all his fault; he was let down and deserted by the people he trusted. It is hard to find one clear culprit, for there were many people involved in the political intrigues. Once again, the intellectual content of the Copernican theory was almost incidental; the conflict was not Christian dogmatism out to stifle science. It was nothing so simple.

Papal Rome in the early seventeenth century was a very volatile place, in which the crucial qualifications for a career were patronage and favour as much as ability, and far more than genuine piety. Few Christians would defend the Catholic Church in this matter. The papal court was a mess of political alliances under the absolute power of the Pope. Galileo, for various reasons as we will see, entered the political games of Rome. He was no novice at political manoeuvres; but in this case, he was not clever enough. It began with his re-entry into public scientific debate in the years following the 1616 prohibition.

In 1618, three comets appeared in the heavens. Grassi, a Jesuit astronomer, gave a public lecture on the comets, which was published. Galileo, in bed with illness and mindful of his prohibition, said nothing. To stay silent, however, was not so easy. For one, there was the matter of professional pride; Galileo, the famous astronomer, had not commented on this major astronomical event. Also, Archduke Leopold of Austria asked Galileo for an answer about the comets. Galileo, still with political obligations at court, had to give one. He wrote under the name of a pupil of his, and then later more fully in a work of his own. As well as presenting his own theory of comets he gave his devastating sarcasm free reign. Grassi was made to look a complete fool, and was none too happy about it. Galileo had created another enemy—and one who was an important Jesuit astronomer. Galileo had managed to alienate one of the most powerful orders within the Catholic Church.

Yet Galileo had won the debate, and with it gained a rising tide of popularity. His book on the comets, *The Assayer*, was loved by court culture.[29] At the same time, he received what must have seemed a great stroke of luck: Cardinal Maffeo Barbarini, who had taken his side in the debate on floating bodies back in 1611, was elected Pope Urban VIII. Urban was renowned for his support of intellectualism and fine culture, and enjoyed giving patronage to those who would bring him credit with their brilliant and innovative ideas. Galileo found out about the election in time to dedicate his book on the comets to the new Pope. Urban was reported to like the book so much he had it read to him during meals.

Galileo's star was on the ascendant again. Travelling to Rome in 1624, he was granted no less than six audiences with the Pope, in which Urban was prepared to discuss Galileo's ideas. Encouraged, Galileo asked for permission to write a full treatise on the Copernican theory. Urban granted it—cautiously, with a strong condition: Galileo must include an argument which Urban framed himself. The argument ran that no physical system can be conclusively proven to be true, for that would limit the power and wisdom of God. God could have created the universe in such a way that man could never discover its secrets. Galileo agreed to the condition.

The result was, after six years, the *Dialogue on the Two Chief World Systems*, probably Galileo's most famous work.[30] The book is a dialogue between three friends— Salviati, the Copernican; Simplicio, the Aristotelian; and Sagredo, the unbiased layman who listens to both sides in order to make up his mind. In this way Galileo managed to present some fairly telling arguments against Aristotelianism as well as what he considered conclusive proof of the Earth's motion—his theory of the tides.[31]

There was great difficulty gaining a license to print the book. Riccardi, the Church official in charge of approving or forbidding the publication of books in Rome, was very cautious. He granted a provisional permission, on the condition that certain changes were made, in particular to the preface and conclusion. The changes were made, but still Riccardi hesitated, and the negotiations dragged on for two years. Finally, under pressure from the Medici Grand-Duke, the license was granted. In February 1632, Galileo's book was printed. Then suddenly Galileo's star halted, and fell. Within a few months the book was banned and all copies seized. Galileo was summoned to Rome to face the Inquisition.

✠

Galileo, it appears, had been fairly confident about the reception of the *Dialogue*. After all, had not the Pope loved *The Assayer*? Had Galileo not included the Pope's argument as requested? Yet Galileo, for whatever reason, had made a mistake. In *The Assayer*, he had been very careful to present Copernicanism as an interesting hypothesis, no more, and it was the intellectual playfulness of it as much as anything else that the Pope had liked. The *Dialogue* was different. Galileo was now showing his colours, and despite lip-service to the 'hypothesis' idea it was clear Galileo was arguing for Copernicanism as *real*. His wit and sarcasm were once again used at the expense of the Aristotelians—and naming the Aristotelian philosopher 'Simplicio' had no less impact then than it does today.[32] Moreover, though Galileo had included the Pope's argument, it was in the mouth of Simplicio, and right at the end of the book. The Pope was, reportedly, furious.

There have been many accounts of Galileo's final trial. Despite his sickness, he was commanded to travel to Rome in winter, and tried before the Inquisition. The main charge against him was that he had disobeyed the command of 1616 'not to defend or hold or teach in any way' Copernicanism. Galileo was surprised (as indeed were many at the trial); for as he remembered, he had only been commanded 'not to defend or hold', and had a signed certificate from Bellarmine with those words. But in what has been seen by some as evidence of conspiracy and by others simply as sloppy bookkeeping, the Inquisition had a record of the 1616 trial—unsigned— which had the extra words 'or teach in any way'.

Galileo's defence throughout the trial was that he had never believed that Copernican theory was *true*, and so was not in defiance of Bellarmine's certificate. It was a lie, of course, but for him a necessary one if he was to have any defence at all. It was not good enough, however, especially given the unsigned document that the Inquisition had unearthed. The judges, or at least a majority of them, were determined to prosecute. They were probably under pressure from the Pope.

Why was the Pope so determined to see Galileo fall? It may have been because he genuinely felt personally insulted by Galileo; or this may have been a front for the political pressure he felt himself under. Urban had been favouring France for some time, and his political bias had angered the Spanish court to the point where he was faced with the possibility of a rupture with Philip VI of Spain. The Spanish were the 'conservative party', strong advocates of the Counter-Reformation and not at all pleased with Urban's sponsoring of radical new intellectuals. Galileo's fall may have been to appease the Spanish; or it could have been that Galileo's enemies in Rome, knowing that the Pope was in an awkward situation any way he turned, worked on his personal vanities to anger him against Galileo. Such puzzles are the stuff that historians delight in;[33] whatever the exact mix of motivations, Galileo's fall appears more or less inevitable. It was inevitable because of the politics involved, *not* because of Christian antipathy to new learning. The Pope, the most powerful figure in Galileo's final downfall, had nothing against the new science; he celebrated it and promoted it. What he objected to was that Galileo did not play the court game as he wanted him to.

Galileo was sentenced as suspected of heresy. This was in many respects an unfair decision; Copernicanism had never been infallibly pronounced heretical.[34] Galileo had actually been *disobedient* rather than heretical, in disobeying the request of 1616. To be ordered for this reason to deny publicly any belief in Copernicanism was harsh, when he could have merely been ordered never to write on the matter again. After all, the *Dialogue* had been licensed for publication. If it really was against the 1616 injunction, it should never have been allowed in print. Riccardi, who granted the licence, had bowed to Medici pressure and Galileo had payed the price. He was the victim of court, academic, and Papal politics.

Nevertheless, Galileo had played his own part in offensive politics over the years, so can hardly be thought of as an innocent victim. He had also disobeyed the request of 1616. Even if it had only been the more lenient 'not to hold or defend', his *Dialogue* clearly disobeyed the spirit of the command. Maybe it was a gamble he took; if so, he lost. He was declared 'vehemently suspected of heresy' and was commanded to 'abjure, curse and detest' his error—that is, he had to state that he did *not* believe that the Earth moved. His *Dialogue* was prohibited and he was sentenced to prison, with three years of a penance of repeating the seven penitential psalms weekly. Yet he was never sent to prison, and his daughter (a nun) was granted permission to say the penitential psalms in his place. Was the Pope thereby admitting Galileo was not really guilty, just a scapegoat? Or were Galileo's court connections still at work? Whatever the reason, Galileo spent the rest of his life working at home, under a type of house arrest, producing solid scientific treatises, but never again enjoying the glittering celebrity he once had.

A few Galileo legends need to be laid to rest. Galileo was never tortured by the Inquisition. The Pope alone, in his official statement concerning Galileo, said that Galileo should be made to abjure on threat of torture; yet this was never part of the judges' sentence, and Galileo was never tortured nor shown the instruments of torture. Galileo needed no prompting to deny the reality of Copernican theory; as stated above, his very defence was that he had never since 1616 thought Copernican theory true. Neither is there any record of Galileo muttering, as he left the courtroom, "and yet it turns". It is unlikely that the clearly frightened Galileo would do anything so foolish—at least in anybody's hearing.

Christianity vs ...?

We have seen that Galileo's story is far more involved—and indeed more interesting—than most caricatures reveal. There is still one more element to add, which is frequently overlooked. At no point did Galileo's story involve *Christianity* opposing anything; it was the Catholic Church, egged on by Aristotelian scholars. What happened when Protestants came across the Copernican theory gives a wider context. There was no widespread horror or outcry against Copernicanism in Protestant countries. It was accepted for what it was: an astronomical theory, of little interest to theologians, but with some technical points to recommend it to astronomers. It was not something to cause a great reaction. There is doubt about whether Calvin ever even heard of the theory.[35] It is unlikely he would have condemned it on biblical grounds. In his commentary on Psalm 136 he was of the opinion that the Holy Spirit "had no intention to teach astronomy".[36] Luther made none but offhand comments about the theory.[37] Those who took the trouble to study Copernicanism were inclined to be mildly in favour of it, if anything. Melancthon, who was responsible for widespread educational reform in Protestant Germany, encouraged astronomy and lectured on Copernicanism. His approach was cautious, but not reactionary; he developed what is known as 'The Wittenberg position', which was influential in Protestant Universities for several decades.[38] While he was not prepared to take on Copernicanism wholeheartedly, he acknowledged its technical improvements over the Ptolemaic theory and was content for his students to study it. It was possible for a member of a Protestant country to be far more enthusiastic—as was Rheticus, the German scholar who was 'converted' to Copernicanism with as much zeal as he gave to religion. Though he did not have many followers, he was certainly not persecuted for his ideas, and indeed continued in a respectable academic career.

Protestant reaction to Copernican theory is a whole research topic in itself, with a considerable literature (though not as much as Galileo). This is not the place to present a comprehensive account. We do, however, need to widen our focus from Galileo and the Catholic Church if we are to make any conclusions about 'Christianity and science'. The Protestant reaction provides a necessary counterpoint to Galileo's condemnation. It is not that Protestantism necessarily had a doctrinal bias towards believing that the earth moved; but if a Protestant *did* wish to accept and defend Copernican theory, he generally had freedom to do so. Without the strict censorship of the Catholic Church, information was more easily disseminated and new ideas more likely to find a hearing in Protestant countries. Protestantism, with its fundamental tenet of individual interpretation of the Bible, did not develop in its institutions the level of control that characterised the Catholic Church. Indeed, after Copernicanism had been suppressed by the Catholic Church, the story was spread far and wide in Protestant polemic against repressive Catholic institutions. All these factors gave Protestant countries an intellectual climate which could be more accepting of Copernicanism than otherwise.[39]

Galileo today

It is now over three hundred and fifty years since Galileo's trial. Since then, his story has been used for its polemic value by groups of all shades of allegiance. A lot of this polemic has been anti-Christian. In response, Christian apologists, either dismissing the incident as 'unfortunate', or citing some of the real historical details behind the anti-Christian myth, have overemphasised the alternative. In other words, it has been common for Christian apologists to draw morals from Galileo's trial that emphasise the true harmony between Christianity and science. Other historical episodes may be used to back this up: the emergence of science from a Christian world view, the numbers of scientists who have also been Christian, and so on. To a certain extent such apologetic is valid; there are many ways in which to demonstrate harmony between Christianity and science.

Yet at a deeper level such polemic has its dangers—as the real story behind Galileo's trial demonstrates. Christians should never allow Christianity to be tied to a secular system of thought. Aristotelianism was very attractive and convincing as an intellectual system, and it gave Christianity a great intellectual boost when the two were 'reconciled'; but Aristotelianism was not Christian, and Christianity should never have been made to depend upon it. The great Aristotelian synthesis left medieval Christianity irrevocably tied to an ultimately faulty philosophy. By the time the flaws in the philosophy were demonstrated, the upholders of the system supposed to be Christian were so steeped in Aristotelianism they were unable to cope with the changes. The result was that Christianity was discredited for something that was nothing to do with it.

The same danger potentially lies before us with theories of modern science, if we are not careful. Modern empirical science is an excellent route to knowledge about our physical universe, and most likely a lot of what it promotes is true. Yet its very success lies in the contingent and revisable nature of its theories. Empirical science is a system which is only ever *probably* true—deliberately so—for by nature it must allow itself to be open to constant revision in the light of new evidence. Science advances by rejection of the old under scrutiny of the new. That is the strength and real value of scientific knowledge.

Christianity, if it really is based on infallible revelation from God, does not need to attach itself to that system and does so at its own peril. There is nothing wrong with demonstrating that any particular scientific theory is compatible with biblical revelation. Such demonstration, however, does not prove the Bible true and should never be made the grounds for accepting biblical truth. In time, the scientific theory will change. Christians must recognise the limits of revealed knowledge, and not connect it to knowledge which is constantly under revision. That is the path to ridicule and disillusionment, when the science moves on and Christians are left behind.

✝

Galileo was not the victim of an anti-science religion. Christianity is not irrevocably tied to a geocentric universe and should never have been stretched to fit an intellectual system in which it appeared so. The Catholic Church was wrong to condemn Galileo, and has certainly suffered in adverse publicity ever since. It is rather unfair, however, that Christianity *per se* is criticised for an incident which was about political necessities and personal grudges far more than it was anything to do with religious issues. The dogmatism which opposed Galileo's innovative science was the dogmatism of the universities, of Aristotelian philosophy which had reigned for centuries and bolstered the intellectual establishment. The theologians who condemned Copernicanism were wrong, but the inflexible opposition to freedom of thought was not theirs.

Yet now Galileo has become an icon of a modern

dogmatism which insists on a war between science and religion, not for any sound intellectual reason but because it suits a modern ideology. If there are historical reasons to propose an inherent clash between science and Christianity, they are not found in Galileo's trial. It is to be hoped that as the mantle of propaganda is lifted from historical truth—as has been done in this century's scholarship on Galileo—that the debate will lose some of its partisan distortion.

ENDNOTES

1   The word 'science' as used here is an anachronism for this era. This is part of the problem for twentieth-century people studying Galileo. The separate disciplines of astronomy and physics, which we now happily group together under the one word, did not enjoy the same conceptual unity in the late sixteenth and early seventeenth centuries.

2   For a summary of the Copernican system and the advantages it had over the Ptolemaic, see section I of Alexander Koyré's *The Astronomical Revolution: Copernicus, Kepler, Borelli*, Hermann, Paris; Methuen, London; Cornell University Press, Ithaca, 1973.

3   John L. Russell 'The Copernican system in Great Britain', pp. 189-239 in Jerzy Dobrzycki (ed.), *The Reception of Copernicus' Heliocentric Theory*, D. Reidel Publishing Company, Dordrecht and Boston, 1972. Reception of the theory in other European countries was similarly luke-warm; see the other essays in this volume for details.

4   Robert S. Westman, "The astronomer's role in the sixteenth century: a preliminary study", *History of Science*, 1980, 28, pp. 105-147, p. 106.

5   Aristotle *De Coelo*. An English translation is available in Milton K. Munitz, *Theories of the Universe: from Babylonian Myth to Modern Science*, The Free Press, New York, 1957 (which also has excepts from Copernicus and Ptolemy). For a summary of

Aristotelian physics and cosmology, see Stephen Toulmin and June Goodfield, *The Fabric of the Heavens*, Penguin Books, Harmondsworth, 1961, ch. 3; or Thomas S. Kuhn, *The Copernican Revolution: Planetary Astronomy in the Development of Western Thought*, Harvard University Press, Cambridge, Massachusetts and London, 1957, ch. 3.

6   Aristotelianism had embedded within it a different conception of the nature of knowledge. There was, it was assumed, a finite amount of knowledge to be gained about the universe, and Aristotle had pretty much done it. There was very little of our modern concept of the progress of knowledge. See William R. Shea, *Galileo's Intellectual Revolution*, Macmillan, London and Basingstoke, p. 31.

7   For discussion of the clash between Aristotle's universe and the new science see Shea (*ibid.*) and Giorgio de Santillana, *The Crime of Galileo*, Heinemann, Melbourne, London and Toronto, 1958.

8   'The Unknown Academician', quoted in Shea (*ibid.*) p. 34 (He was actually Arturo Pannochieschi de' Conti d'Elci, the overseer of Pisa University).

9   Quoted in Shea (*ibid.*) pp. 34-35. di Grazia was a professor in philosophy at Pisa.

10   A professor of medicine could earn twice as much as a professor of mathematics. Westman, *op. cit.*, p. 119.

11   Before Copernicus, there was some justification for being pessimistic about the capacity of mathematical astronomy to address reality—the Ptolemaic model was a mathematical labyrinth. Adjustments were made to fit observations of individual planets at the price of increasing complexity. It was not developed as a physical system. See Kuhn, *op. cit.*, ch. 2.

12   In 1605 Galileo published a satirical dialogue criticising the work of one of the leading Aristotelian scholars, Lodovico delle Colombe. He also ridiculed the ranking professor of philosophy at Padua, Cesare Creminini, who had attacked him publicly.

13   This is the basis of the thesis developed in Mario Biagioli, *Galileo, Courtier: The Practice of Science in the Culture of Absolutism*, The University of Chicago Press, Chicago and London, 1993.

14   It is actually inaccurate to say that the discovery of the moons of Jupiter 'proved' Copernican theory. It provided a

strong argument against the Aristotelian cosmology in which everything in the heavens revolved around the earth, but it was still a long step to confirming a Copernican system.

15   Galileo's first salary as a mathematician at the university of Pisa was 160 scudi per year. The court salary of 1000 scudi was about three times that of any highly paid artist or engineer (Biagioli, *ibid.*, p. 104). For an analysis of the political rhetoric Galileo used to obtain his court position, see Biagioli pp. 103-157 and also his 'Galileo the emblem-maker', *Isis*, 1990, *81*, pp. 230-58.

16   It was around the same time that Lodovico delle Colombe published *Against the Earth's motion* in opposition to Galileo's celestial discoveries.

17   See Biagioli *ibid.* pp. 159-169 for a fuller description of Galileo's life and responsibilities at court.

18   It was during this debate that the previously quoted comments on mathematics were made.

19   See Shea *op. cit* ch. 2 and Biagioli *op. cit.* pp. 170-209 for analysis of this debate. The debate is interesting for its reflection of the opposing beliefs about nature as much as the detail of hydrostatics involved.

20   Galileo had been given a banquet in his honour by the mathematicians at the Jesuit Collegio Romano in Rome in 1611.

21   For an account of the personalities and motivations involved in the 1616 incident, see Olaf Pederson, 'Galileo and the Council of Trent: the Galileo affair revisited', *Journal of the History of Astronomy*, 1983, *114*, pp. 1-29; , Jerome J. Langford, *Galileo, Science and the Church*, University of Michigan Press, 1976; Richard S. Westfall, *Essays on the Trial of Galileo*, Vatican University Publications, 1989; and Santillana, *op. cit.*

22   Olaf Pederson, *ibid.*, pp. 6-8

23   Peter Dear, 'The church and the new philosophy', in Stephen Pumfrey (ed.), *Science, Culture and Popular Belief in Renaissance Europe*, Manchester University Press, Manchester and New York, 1991, pp. 119-139.

24   With rather more sophistication, these types of interpretations of Galileo's actions have appeared in the historical literature. Westfall *op. cit.* and Langford *op. cit.* lean towards a pugnacious Galileo, Westfall's one-word description being 'insufferable';

Pederson *op. cit.*, and especially Stillman Drake (*Galileo*, Oxford University Press, Oxford, 1980) emphasise Galileo's commitment to his ideals of truth; Joseph Pitt's Galileo is merely a scientific opportunist who pushed his luck too far ('The heavens and earth: Bellarmine and Galileo', in Peter Barker and Roger Ariew (eds), *Revolution and Continuity: Essays in the History and Philosophy of Early Modern Science*, The Catholic University of America Press, Washington D. C., 1991, pp. 131-142).

25 This background information about Bellarmine is largely taken from Westfall, *op. cit.*, ch. 1.

26 The Catholic church as a whole had put unprecedented restrictions on freedom to interpret the Bible in response to the Reformation schism. This was influential in the 1616 decision. See Westfall *ibid.*

27 Quoted in Westfall, *ibid.*, p. 9.

28 See Westfall *ibid..* An English translation of the letter can be found in Maurice A. Finocchiaro, *The Galileo Affair: A Documentary History*, University of California Press, Berkeley, Los Angeles and London, 1989.

29 As it turns out Galileo was mistaken about the nature of comets, perhaps because he did not have time for detailed observation. Galileo's theory was that comets were merely optical illusions produced by refraction of the sun's rays in the upper atmosphere. What made his book so popular was not the theory *per se* but the skill and wit with which he discussed it. For an English translation of the book, see Stillman Drake (trans. and ed.), *The Controversy on the Comets of 1618*, Pennsylvania University Press, Philadelphia, 1960.

30 There are innumerable analyses of this work. The most detailed would have to be Maurice A. Finocchiaro, *Foundations of Logic and Scientific Method*, D. Reidel Publishing Company, Dordrecht, Boston, and London, 1980. For an English translation of the book, see Galileo Galilei, *Dialogue Concerning the Two Chief World Systems, Ptolemaic and Copernican*, trans. Stillman Drake, University of California Press, Berkeley, 1967.

31 Johannes Kepler, the famous German astronomer who discovered the elliptical orbit of the planets, had already explained tides in terms of the moon's attraction, but Galileo rejected the

notion. He instead attempted to explain tides purely in terms of the Earth's motion. He used the analogy of a barge; as the barge starts or stops, the water inside it sloshes to one side or the other. See Harold L. Burstyn, 'Galileo's attempt to prove that the Earth moves', *Isis*, 1962, *53*, pp. 161-85.

32 There was a real ancient Greek commentator on Aristotle called Simplicio, but the double meaning was hardly accidental.

33 Richard Westfall *op. cit.* blames the Pope's personal anger rather than political pressure, as, it seems, does Drake (*Galileo op. cit.*); Biagioli *op. cit.* considers the political problems dominant; William Wallace ('Galileo and the Church', in David C. Lindberg and Ronald L. Numbers, *God and Nature: Historical Essays on the Encounter between Christianity and Science*, University of California Press, Berkeley, Los Angeles and London, 1986, pp. 114-135) writes of the political situation with a Hermetic tinge, as do the rather more speculative E. A. Gosselin and L. S. Lerner, 'Galileo and the long shade of Bruno', *Archives Internationales d'Histoire des Sciences*, 1975, *25*, pp. 223-46; Santillana *op. cit.* thinks that the Jesuits, angered by Galileo, aroused the embattled Urban's fury by claiming that Galileo's book ridiculed him. One book caused a great stir by claiming that all previous theories are wrong, and in fact the trial was about Galileo being under suspicion of denying the doctrine of transubstantiation, and nothing to do with Copernicanism at all. This new reading has not been well accepted (see, for instance, Westfall's review in *op. cit.* ch. 4; or Vincenzo Ferrone and Massimo Firpo, 'From inquisitors to microhistorians: a critique of Pietro Redondi's *Galileo Eretico*' (review article), *The Journal of Modern History*, 1986, *58*, pp. 485-524; the book in question is Pietro Redondi, *Galileo Heretic*, trans. Raymond Rosenthal, The Penguin Press, London, 1987).

34 See Langford, *op. cit.*, p. 155.

35 See Edward Rosen, 'Calvin's attitude toward Copernicus', *Journal of the History of Ideas*, 1960, pp. 431-441; Robert White 'Calvin and Copernicus: the problem considered' *Calvin Theological Journal*, 1980, *15*, pp. 233-43; and Christopher B. Kaiser, 'Calvin, Copernicus and Castellio', *Calvin Theological Journal*, 21, 1986, pp. 5-31

36 John Calvin, *Commentary on the Book of Psalms* vol. 5, James

Anderson (ed. and trans.), Wm B. Eerdmans Publishing Company, Grand Rapids, 1949, p. 184.

37   The one famous comment is recorded in Luther, 'Table Talk', *Luther's Works* vol. 54, Theodore G. Tappert (ed. and trans.), Fortress Press, Philadelphia, 1967, pp. 358-359; for discussion of the likely veracity of this record, see Wilhelm Norlind, 'Copernicus and Luther: a critical study', *Isis*, 1953, *44*, pp. 273-276.

38   See Robert S. Westman, 'The Melanchthon circle, Rheticus, the Wittenberg Interpretation of the Copernican theory', *Isis*, 1975, *66*, pp. 165-93.

39   See John Hedley Brooks, *Science and Religion: Some Historical Perspectives*, Cambridge University Press, Cambridge, 1991, pp. 94-109, for discussion of these issues.

2.
Miracles and rational belief
Roger White

*E*VER SINCE DAVID Hume proclaimed that "no human testimony can have such force as to prove a miracle and make it a just foundation for any such system of religion",[1] the subject of miraculous events has been of fascination to philosophers. Have any miracles ever occurred? It would seem on the face of it that such a question can only be answered by a careful analysis of the evidence for specific cases. Yet Hume and others argue that such inquiry is pointless from the start. It is argued that it is impossible even *in principle* to have sufficient evidence for a miracle. Moreover, even if we can establish a certain event has taken place, we can draw no supernatural conclusions, hence we cannot establish that it is 'miraculous' in any interesting sense. Rather than defend the occurrence and significance of any particular miracle, my focus will be on these preliminary philosophical issues. My purpose is to defend the appropriateness of empirical investigation of miracle reports by arguing that we can, in principle, have sufficient evidence to establish the occurrence of a miracle, and that such knowledge can provide evidence for religious beliefs.

First we should be clear on the sort of events we are

concerned with. But let's note that there is little to be gained by sceptics or believers fussing over the definition of the term 'miracle'. When all has been said and done about defining the term 'miracle', nothing has been said about what has or has not actually happened. The question of whether or not, given certain definitions of terms, the bodily resurrection of Jesus is labelled a 'miracle' is insignificant—you can call it a 'banana' if you wish—what is interesting is *did it actually happen?* and this cannot be answered by playing with words.

For instance, it is often suggested that for an event to count as genuinely miraculous it must involve the violation of a law of nature by an act of direct intervention by God.[2] This has lead to much confusion and pointless discussion. For instance, you can come up against logical impossibility. You can define a miracle as a violation as a law of nature, and then argue that since true laws of nature describe what actually takes place, miracles by definition do not occur. While this very conveniently removes the possibility of the miraculous (on this particular conception of miracles) it tells us nothing about whether Jesus rose from the dead. It merely tells us that the term 'miracle' can be so defined as to be logically incoherent, like 'square circle'. Such a definition adds nothing to our discussion of whether particular claimed events really took place. I propose to sidestep these conceptual issues by focusing on a paradigm case of a miracle rather than offer any definition. The resurrection of Jesus surely counts as a miracle if anything does, and it is events of this type that we are concerned with in any serious debate about miracles.

It has been suggested by others that although miracles are not *logically* impossible, they are *physically* impossible. That is, it is claimed that miracles necessarily involve overriding true laws by a supernatural power. *But*, it is then argued, how can we know that any event is really an act of God, and not something which nature could bring about *unaided*, so to speak? Antony Flew presents the point in this manner:

> The natural scientist, confronted with some occurrence inconsistent with a proposition previously believed to express a law of nature, can find in this disturbing inconsistency no ground whatever for proclaiming that the particular law of nature has been supernaturally overridden. On the contrary, the new discovery is simply a reason for his conceding that he had previously been wrong in thinking that the proposition thus confuted, did indeed express a true law; it is also a reason for his resolving to search again for the law which really does obtain.[3]

It is, however, not true that the scientist has "no ground whatever" for coming to conclusions about the supernatural in such a case. It may be that to salvage the natural law requires just too many *ad hoc* adjustments. For example, the natural law that people die and stay dead may be amended by the clause 'except when the person's name begins with the letter J, he claims to be God and founds a major western religion.' Then the scientist may proclaim, 'So there, it is not really a miracle after all, for it fits well with the laws of nature!' In practice, of course, a competent scientist will find it extremely difficult to make such a bizarre amendment; or to amend such general laws at all, without overturning vast amounts of well-established theory.[4]

Objections such as these have led to a type of double-dealing in arguments about miracles. Broadly speaking, there have been two main arguments levelled against the belief in miracles. Firstly, there is the epistemological problem raised by Hume: that miracles by their very nature are so improbable that no amount of evidence could possibly justify belief in one (we will be examining this problem shortly). Secondly, it is argued that science is advancing, so what may now seem to be an inexplicable event will one day be explained scientifically, and shown not to be improbable in the circumstances.[5] Many philosophers have seen these problems as the two horns of a dilemma which makes rational belief in miracles impossible. The believer in miracles is thought to be in a real fix. Caught between on the one hand the inductive strength of scientific evidence ruling out miraculous events, and on the other, the onward march of science and its ability to explain all phenomena no matter how strange, there seems to be no place left for miracles. This leaves the sceptic with a happy 'heads-I-win-tails-you-lose' argument against the miraculous. Events which *do* seem miraculous can be dismissed as being too improbable to be rationally believed to have occurred; and if they have occurred, well, science can explain them anyway.[6]

However although either one of the above arguments may apply to a *particular* event, they cannot *both* apply to the *same* event. The following illustration should make this clear. Suppose a friend were to say to me "I saw a faith healer last night and my back is feeling a lot better!" Although I am sceptical that a supernatural event has taken place, I am hardly going to respond "No! I can't believe that your back feels better". I have no doubt that her back feels better, but I do not believe this is a miracle. Given our modern understanding of psychosomatic illness, the event is far from inexplicable and in fact quite probable, and it is for this reason that I have no doubt that it happened. But now suppose tomorrow she says to me "I flew to the moon and back this morning by flapping my arms". In this case it would be ludicrous to say "Did you? I'm sure there is an adequate scientific explanation for that". Rather, I would be extremely sceptical that the event took place, and the reason for the scepticism is precisely that not only is there no scientific explanation for it, but it seems highly improbable that there could even be one, given our present understanding of physics. If I believed it at all likely that such an event falls under the scope of our present or future scientific understanding (in such a way as to increase its probability), then I would have less reason to be so sceptical about it.

The fallacy of the 'heads-I-win-tails-you-lose' argument should be evident. We simply cannot have it both ways. If I am to be sceptical about my friend flying to the moon, I do so on the basis that I have extremely good scientific evidence that it could not happen. As I am presented with more testimonial or empirical evidence that it did happen, I will stubbornly maintain that it is more likely not to have happened, given the scientific evidence against it. The further I am pushed with evidence supporting the event, the stronger must be my insistence that such an event could not be naturally explained, if I am to retain my scepticism. Now *if* (and this is a big if) the evidence became so strong that it was more rational for me to conclude that the event had in fact taken place, then I could not simply leap to the other end of the spectrum and say, "Well yes, so you did fly to the moon, but there must be a perfectly adequate natural explanation for it". For if it were at all probable that such an event could be explained, then I would have no basis by which to be so stubbornly sceptical of the event.

It does the sceptic no good to define himself out of believing anything. If something highly improbable, such as the resurrection of Jesus, nevertheless happened, it cannot be explained away by insisting that it is not a miracle. That merely brings us back to the word-games with which we started.

✻

The focus on violations of physical law and divine intervention seems misguided. First, given the statistical nature of modern physical theories it is not at all clear that 'miraculous' events do strictly contradict physical laws—but this renders such events not the least bit less astonishing. A person rising from the dead, or water turning into wine, is highly unusual and amazing however you describe it. Second, it is not clear what is the relevance of the notion of divine intervention. On one view of the relation between God and creation, God is continually controlling and sustaining every part of creation. On this view *every* event is an act of God. All talk of 'overriding of laws' or 'interventions into the natural order' assumes a conception of God and the world which has little relevance in this context. The laws of nature, whatever else we might say about them, can be seen as descriptions of the regular ways in which God acts in the world. A miracle, then, is not a supernatural event in contrast to 'nature'; it is God acting one way as opposed to all the other ways in which he acts. God does not have to poke his fingers into the natural mechanisms of the world to perform a miracle, he merely acts in a way different from the usual course for a specific purpose.

At any rate, we need not dwell on these matters. Christians assert first and foremost that Jesus did in fact rise from the dead. The metaphysical details of how this occurred are entirely secondary. There are no interesting difficulties here to pursue. Clearly if there is a God who created the universe and gave human beings life, he would have little difficulty in giving life to a man after his death. Once again, the interesting question here is whether this actually happened and what we can conclude from it.

Objections to miracles

Let us turn then to consider our first serious objection to belief in miracles. In David Hume's classic discussion, we find an intriguing argument that we could not possibly have sufficient evidence that a miracle has occurred. Hume's argument is a matter of balancing probabilities. When we consider testimonial evidence for a miracle, there are broadly speaking, two possible conclusions to draw: (1) The person giving the testimony is lying or has been deceived, or (2) the testimony is correct and the miracle occurred. Now miracles by their very nature are extremely improbable, so (2) is doubtful; but people are known to lie and be deceived, so (1) is more likely. Hence, as "a wise man...proportions his belief to the evidence",[7] he should, on the balance of probabilities, believe (1).

But are these probabilities correctly assigned? The crucial aspect of Hume's argument is the use of observed relative frequencies of events to assign probabilities. According to Hume:

> All probability, then, supposes an opposition of experiments...we must balance the opposite experiments where they are opposite, and deduct the smaller number from the greater in order to know the exact force of the superior evidence.[8]

Taking the case of the resurrection, we know the following two propositions:
(a) All observed dead people have stayed dead
(b) Not all people tell the truth

These two propositions give a certain probability for the following two:

(a') Jesus stayed dead
(b') The disciples spoke truly

Statement (a) confers an extremely high probability on (a'), whereas (b) confers a slightly lower probability on (b'). Hence (a') is more probable, and should be believed.

This is Hume's argument in a nutshell. It is one that cannot be easily dismissed. Note that Hume's argument is epistemological (dealing with what we can know). He is concerned with the conditions under which it is *reasonable to believe* that a miracle has occurred. He is not making the silly claim that we can know that miracles such as the resurrection are *impossible*. Indeed Hume would be the first to deny this. We should also note that we all do dismiss most reports of miracles for the very reason that, all things considered, it seems more likely that the reporter is deceitful or deceived than that the event occurred. The question is whether it should *always* turn out that the weight of evidence falls on (1). If that were true, then we need never again consider the evidence for a claimed miracle, as it would always be more likely that people were lying or deceived—although to conclude that we need not look at the evidence would be rather ironic after agreeing that 'a wise man proportions his belief to the evidence'.

How do we determine whether the balance of probabilities will always lead us to conclude (1)? We need to understand how Hume went about assigning probabilities. The idea behind Hume's approach is that in assigning probabilities to (say) the outcome of an event, we should consider the event as a member of a certain class of similar events, and ask in what proportion of the events of this class was there an outcome of the relevant type. That is, out of all the times this thing was tried, how many times did it happen? The more times it happened in the past, the more likely it is to happen again. This principle has a certain limited application. My confidence that my car will start when I turn the key, should be based in part upon the frequency with which it started upon turning the key in the past.

But Hume's claim that this is all there is to the assignment of probabilities is hopelessly simplistic. The major problem is that of finding the appropriate class of events with which to judge the frequencies of outcomes. Every event is a member of any number of classes of events. Depending on the class, there will be different proportions of a certain type of outcome occurring. So Hume's method does not give us an absolute probability for an outcome of an event.

For instance, suppose I am trying to decide whether to take up hang-gliding or lawn bowls. I want to know which is more dangerous, so I determine how many people from each sport have died. It turns out that a greater proportion of people who play lawn bowls have died each year than those who do hang-gliding. It is more probable, I conclude, that I will die if I take up lawn bowls than if I take up hang-gliding. (In this I have reasoned exactly as Hume does.)

However I may be considering the wrong class of events. It might be pointed out that if I take a narrower class of events—namely, a person under thirty playing lawn bowls—only a small proportion of these will be accompanied by death. The point would still hold even if no one under thirty had tried lawn bowls or hang-gliding. Even so, how do I decide that 'under thirty' is the relevant category? It may be important to note the low fatality rate among people under thirty in general, but this alone will not distinguish between the hang-gliding and lawn bowling cases. At any rate, it is not clear whether I should consider the people under thirty throughout the world, or in my house, or those with red hair, or those that don't smoke, and so forth. Clearly our judgements as to which classes of events are relevant for assigning probabilities must involve judgements about the *causally* relevant features of an event. But then of course our judgements concerning causal relations are based in part on observed statistical regularities. In any realistic case, the matter gets exceedingly complex and there is no simple formula for making judgements of probabilities.

My purpose in the preceding discussion has been merely to bring out some of the complexities involved in using observed frequencies of event outcomes to make judgements of probability. Given that there is no systematic method for drawing probabilistic conclusions from frequency data,[9] and indeed it is doubtful that there even could be, it becomes extremely implausible that a conclusion as general and as strong as

Hume's could possibly be defended. At any rate, Hume has certainly given us insufficient grounds for accepting it. We cannot conclude that it is always more likely for people to lie or be deceived, than for a miracle to have occurred.

How to decide whether a miracle is plausible

Hume, then, fails to show that we could not *possibly* have sufficient evidence that a miracle has occurred. That is, he has not shown it is *always* more likely for people to lie or be deceived. This is not surprising, given the strength of the claim; it is hard to prove that anything is *always*, without exception, the case. Nonetheless, the sceptic may still argue that it is extremely *difficult* to establish the occurrence of a miracle. However, the sceptic is in danger of being over-confident here. Of course to establish that a miracle has occurred, we would want something fairly convincing; but we need not assume that miracle reports will always be hard to believe. To thoroughly address this point we would need to look at specific cases. Here I will just make some general points about how to approach the matter.

1. Is it likely that a miracle would happen?

If we are presented with a report of a miracle, can we take the report seriously? Is it ever innately probable that such a thing would be true? The important factor here will be our theological presuppositions. The likelihood of an event such as the resurrection varies greatly relative to different sets of background beliefs.

Certain background assumptions, such as the existence of God, may raise the probability of miracles significantly. If I have reason (on other grounds) to believe that Jesus was no ordinary man, my expectancy of his fate after death will be affected. We must take this seriously, for it is often glossed over in discussions of miracles (it is not taken seriously by Hume). It is in an important sense quite unrealistic to discuss whether a miracle happened, without reference to anything else. For *if* God is real, and *if* he promised a messiah who would not be held by the grave, *then* the claim that one particular person rose from the grave becomes more likely. The background beliefs that a person holds make a real difference to the likelihood of a particular event.

Imagine if someone had tried to convince the eighteenth-century Hume of the findings of twentieth-century science; nuclear physics, relativity, space exploration and so on. Given his existing knowledge, he probably would not have believed any such thing, and it would have been highly irrational of him if he had. For us, with additional background information, we do not find the existence of space shuttles implausible and so can accept that they exist (even though most of us have never seen one). The likelihood of a single piece of information being true is very much affected by what else the person already holds as true.

It is only reasonable, then, that an atheist should consider the resurrection extremely unlikely, a theist somewhat more likely and someone who already believes that Jesus was God incarnate should find the event plausible even before considering further evidence (note such judgements have nothing to do with statistical regularities of past events). The *truth* of whether Jesus rose from the dead is not in any sense relative to what people believe—he either did rise or he didn't. But there is an important sense in which the *rationality* of a person's belief that Jesus rose is relative to her background beliefs. Of course we might raise questions about the truth or rationality of these background beliefs—or we may want to begin to persuade a person to take on certain background beliefs. In any case, we can ask *given* that she believes this and that, what attitude should she hold to the resurrection?

There are two consequences to this. First, while consideration of the views of others is important in any inquiry, ultimately your judgements must be based on your own background beliefs not anyone else's. This might seem trivial, but one implication is that your success or lack of success in convincing others of your own views should have little bearing on what you come to believe. In special cases, such as when everyone around disagrees with me on one point while we agree on so many others, I might be forced to wonder if my reasoning has gone astray. But this is not the case in most discussions. I might have available to me more information than those around me. We typically find that there are a wide variety of views and people are coming from vastly different backgrounds. It is sometimes insisted that the *burden of proof* rests on those who affirm that miracles have occurred. It is not clear just what this amounts to, but if it entails that one should be able to convince others of a view before one accepts it then this is clearly wrong. My inability to convince someone may be due to a failure to find points of agreement on which to begin discussion. I may simply not know of any argument for my position which begins from assumptions which others accept. Either way, this is of no concern to me in figuring out what is true.

We often speak of *objectivity* as a virtue in inquiry. If by this we mean not being swayed by prejudices and emotions which we know are not aimed at the truth, then this is good advice. But there is an important sense in which an appropriate line of reasoning is relative to the subject who is reasoning. My judgements are formed by integrating new data into my own view of the world and having it face the tribunal of my own set of background beliefs. These background beliefs are certainly open to revision, but such revisions are made in the light of my overall view of the world. If I believe there is a God who created and controls all of nature, if it strikes me that Jesus was no ordinary man, these claims can and should play a role in my judging the likelihood of Jesus' resurrection. It may be appropriate to question these beliefs, but we should be under no illusion that my judgements of the likelihood of a miracle should take into consideration only those facts that are uncontroversial.

The belief that the world was created and is continually controlled by an almighty being not only makes the occurrence of a miracle more probable, it provides one with an entirely different framework in which to consider the case. For when we are dealing with the actions of a *personal* agent, and not merely the blind forces of nature, such features as the *purpose* and *significance* of the event become relevant. If I were to hear that a friend has quit university and has been living in a tree for some weeks, I might find the story too hard to believe. The problem is not that she could not do this, it just seems unlikely given her behaviour in the past. But when I hear that she is protesting the logging of rain forests, the story makes more sense and is far more plausible. The analogy is loose, but in a similar way God has no difficulty in bringing about any event at all, but an understanding of the *purpose* that God might have in bringing about a miracle, can make such an event far more believable.[10]

The second point to draw from the relativity of rational belief which I have been stressing, is that we should have a modest view about the force of our *arguments*. On the one hand we have Christian evangelists insisting that they can *prove* beyond a shadow of a doubt that Jesus rose from the dead, and on the other, sceptics insisting that they can completely demolish such a claim. Both have an unrealistic view of the issue. Sometimes our arguments fail to convince others due to their stubbornness, ignorance, irrationality or fear of the consequences. But often it is just that considerations that we find compelling are not so to someone with a radically different set of background beliefs. We might try to challenge these other beliefs but we will face the same problem again. This is not to suggest that discussion on these matters is not worthwhile. Arguments help draw our attention to logical relations between various propositions and hence guide us in adjusting our overall view of things in a coherent way. The cumulative effect of such discussions, together with various experiences and learning may be that someone changes her views in a radical way (such as to believe in the resurrection) but we should not overestimate the significance of a set of arguments alone.

2. Can we have evidence that a miracle happened?

Let us turn now to the other side of the evidence: the testimonies and other external historical details which support the occurrence of a miracle. I want to consider the force of such evidence even for someone with no prior belief in God and hence for whom miracles are extremely improbable. According to Hume, the probability of the miracle having happened will be low, and the probability that the witnesses were wrong will be high. Is that true?

First note that we cannot afford to be too sceptical in general about knowledge based on testimony, for so much of what we believe comes to us this way. Indeed even our evidence that miracles are improbable is largely based on what we have been told. Very few of us have directly observed what happens as people die, nor do many of us understand the biological process of death. What we do know comes largely from what our parents or our teachers or our textbooks told us. So any general scepticism about the reliability of testimony would tend also to weaken the case *against* miracles.[11]

Moreover, we must be aware of the relevance of different pieces of evidence. It is true that a great many bridges have collapsed throughout history and throughout the world, yet this does not make me doubt the reliability of the Sydney Harbour Bridge. Knowledge of features specific to *that* bridge might support an extremely low probability of it failing. Similarly, factors specific to a particular set of reports might give them much greater credibility than reports in general. In determining how likely it is that a report is accurate, it is often useful to consider what it would take for the report to be false, in *this* particular case given the specific details we know. Might the reporters have lied? Did they have a motive to, or did they have a motive not to (say, if they were under threat of persecution)? Were they just mistaken? How might such a mistake have come about? It is not that we must be able to tell a convincing story about *how* the reports could be false, in order to conclude that they are. But by focusing only on the improbability of the miracle we can fail to notice just how improbable the alternative is also.

Furthermore, there is not only testimonial evidence to consider, but further historical facts which require explanation. One example often cited in the case of the resurrection is the astonishing emergence of Christianity in Jerusalem, shortly after Jesus' crucifixion—a faith which seems to have been founded on belief in his resurrection. Events such as these (about which there is no doubt at all) may lend support to the overall case for a miracle. For such an event is improbable on the assumption that the miracle did *not* occur—but it is to be expected on the assumption that it did. That is, if there was no resurrection, the emergence of Christianity is highly improbable; but if there was a resurrection, the emergence of Christianity is very likely. What we have overall is a complex web of facts and hypotheses, with various evidential links of the form 'if A happened, then it is most likely that B'. So each hypothesis we consider will be in tension with other elements of the web.

We might reason for instance that if it were the case that Jesus' body was still rotting in the tomb, then it is most likely that the authorities would have displayed it in order to crush the Christian faith (for they had every motive to). And if they *had* produced the corpse, then it is almost certain that Christianity would have been destroyed (for the early Christians believed in nothing less than the literal bodily resurrection). Given that the faith was not destroyed, it is implausible that his body was still in the tomb. Of course there is a whole lot more to consider than this. Our inquiry should aim at achieving a theory with the best overall explanatory coherence. Looked at in this way, we can see just how inadequate was Hume's account of the balancing of probabilities.

A final point to note concerning evidence is just how powerful the cumulative effect of independent pieces of evidence can be. It is a familiar point in the case of forensic evidence, that while the individual facts considered in isolation lend only meagre support to a case, their combined effect may be great. There are good theoretical grounds for the phenomenon. A crucial factor in the force of a piece of evidence for a hypothesis is the *prior* likelihood of that evidence. The prior likelihood is how likely it is that the evidence would have happened in any case, whether or not the hypothesis is true.

When we are considering eye-witness accounts as evidence for an event, we need to ask how likely it is that the account would have been made if the event actually did not happen. If the reporter has a reputation for always saying the same thing regardless of the truth, then his reports have a high prior likelihood. That is, the reporter would have said what he said anyway, regardless of what actually happened. On the other hand, if there is no reason to think he has lied, or if it is extremely unlikely he would have lied, then the report has a lower prior likelihood. The same goes for any piece of evidence. If it would have happened anyway, we don't take it as evidence for the event. If it is extremely unlikely it would have happened without the event, then we take it as strong evidence for the event.

Now whatever the prior likelihood of each particular piece of evidence may be, the prior likelihood of *all* of them all obtaining (say, of several people reporting the very same event) will often be extremely low.[12] That means, if there are several independent pieces of evidence, they can add together to make a very strong case for the event.[13] Contrary to Hume, then, there is no guarantee in advance that the probability of the miracle given our total evidence will be low. If we want to be sure whether a miracle occurred, we have no choice but to look carefully at the evidence.

Can a miracle provide evidence for religious belief?

Finally, we turn to consider whether the occurrence of a miracle can provide evidence for religious beliefs. If we can demonstrate that a miracle happened, does that give us grounds for accepting (say) Christianity? Much of the discussion about violation of the laws of nature which I earlier dismissed addresses this point. It is argued that if miracles are not in some way contrary to natural laws, then they are not significantly distinguished from everyday events, and there is no special reason to believe that a supernatural power is involved. Even if we could demonstrate that this 'miracle' happened, there is no reason to say it is supernatural; it is just another (albeit strange) instance of the natural world. Antony Flew argues that

> It is only and precisely insofar as it is something really transcendent—something, so to speak, which nature by herself could not contrive—that such an occurrence could force us to conclude that some supernatural power is being revealed.[14]

In a similar vein, J. L. Mackie[15] argues that the believer in miracles is stuck with the awkward task of not only arguing that a particular event occurred, but also that this event violated a genuine law of nature, if he is to claim that the event is of some supernatural significance. And these two tasks are difficult to achieve together.

First of all, we note that both Flew and Mackie are assuming a dichotomy between natural and supernatural that is not necessary, as already discussed above. Moreover, regardless of whether we are "forced", what we want to know is what conclusions might the occurrence *support* and how might it support them. And if we step back for a moment and consider a specific case, the objections of Flew and Mackie are not compelling. Surely it is just plain obvious that *if* we were to know that Jesus rose from the dead, this would provide some support for the truth of Christianity.

Ironically, the fact that miracles provide evidence for religious hypotheses follows directly from a principle which Mackie himself has defended, and requires no assumptions about violations of natural laws.[16] The principle states that a piece of evidence raises the likelihood of a hypothesis whenever that evidence is more likely given the hypothesis. The principle follows from the axioms of probability and is central to common-sense reasoning. Footprints in the dirt confirm that someone has been walking there since the footprints are more likely to be there given that someone did walk there. The sound of the siren suggests that there is a fire nearby, for a siren is more likely to be heard when there is a fire nearby.

Flew and Mackie both agree that while miracles are extremely improbable, their occurrence is more likely on the assumption that God exists. And as we discussed above, more specific religious beliefs may raise further the likelihood of a miracle. So it follows from Mackie's criterion of confirmation that the occurrence of miracles may confirm religious beliefs. For instance, since the resurrection of Jesus is far more likely on the assumption that he was divine, the resurrection, if we knew it to have occurred, would confirm Jesus' divinity. Of course it does not *prove* it, but it does provide substantial support.

✝

To sum up then, the philosophical objections to miracles fail. We can, in principle, have sufficient evidence to believe that a miracle has occurred. And if we did, this could provide evidence for religious beliefs. Nothing I have argued should increase our credulity about miracles in general, before considering specific evidence. It may well turn out that there is insufficient evidence for miracles. Or it might not. I have merely sought to remove some of the philosophical mistakes which can impede a serious investigation of the evidence. As to whether any miracles have occurred—let the reader be the judge.

ENDNOTES

1   David Hume, *On Human Nature and the Understanding*, Collier books, New York, 1962, p. 133.

2   This definition derives from Hume's classic discussion in *On Human Nature*, *ibid*. Interestingly, Hume sees no conceptual difficulties with this definition. He is concerned with our

evidence for the events themselves, rather than the conceptual and metaphysical issues.

3   A. Flew, 'Miracles', *Encyclopaedia of Philosophy*, 1972, vol 5. p. 349.

4   This point has been developed further by several philosophers including R. Swinburne, *The Concept of Miracle*, Macmillan, London, 1970, pp. 23-33; M. Boden, 'Miracles and scientific explanation', *Ratio*, 1967, 11, pp. 137-44; and R. H. Holland, 'The miraculous', *American Philosophical Quarterly*, 1965, 2, pp. 46-51.

5   See for example G. Robinson, 'Miracles', *Ratio*, 1967, 9, pp. 155-66; and M. L. Diamond, 'Miracles', *Religious Studies*, 1972, 9, pp. 307-24.

6   The heads-I-win-tails-you-lose approach is a surprisingly popular one. See for example Flew 'Miracles', *op. cit.*, 00, 347-50; Mackie *op. cit.*, pp. 13-29 and J. Hospers, *An Introduction to Philosophical Analysis*, Routledge and Kegan Paul, London, 1956, pp. 450-54.

7   Hume, *op. cit*, p. 116.

8   Hume, *op. cit..*, p. 116.

9   Perhaps there is a notion of probability which is defined in terms of actual relative frequencies of event outcomes. But the notion we are concerned with is that of a *degree of reasonable belief* in the light of evidence, for we are in the end concerned with the rationality of belief in miracles. It is bridging the gap between frequency data and rational belief which is a subtle and complex matter.

10   For a further discussion on this point see C. S. Lewis, *Miracles: A Preliminary Study*, Fontana Books, London, 1967, pp. 111-67.

11   C. D. Broad makes a similar point in "Hume's Theory of the Credibility of Miracles", in A. Sesonske, and N. Fleming, (eds), *Human Understanding: Studies in the Philosophy of David Hume*, Wadsworth Publishing Co., California, 1965, pp. 95-6.

12   This will depend of course on how independent we take the various pieces of evidence to be. If there is some suspicion that the reports were copied, their combined effect is diminished.

13   Using the calculus of probabilities we can see why this is the case. If for simplicity we assume that the elements of our set of evidential statements $\{E_1, E_2,..., E_n\}$ are entirely independent, then the probability of a miracle M on this total evidence is given by the formula

$$P(M|E_1 \& E_2 \&...\&E_n) = \frac{P(M) \times P(E_1|M) \times P(E_2|M) \times...\times(E_n|M)}{P(E_1) \times P(E_2) \times...\times P(E_n)}$$

The crucial point here is that the value of the denominator $P(E_1) \times P(E_2) \times...\times P(E_n)$ will become very small very quickly as we increase n, regardless of the individual probabilities of the evidential statements. Hence the value of the expression will increase dramatically as we obtain new pieces of independent evidence.

14   A. Flew, "Miracles", *Encyclopedia of Philosophy*, 1972 ed., vol. 5, p. 348.
15   J. L. Mackie, *The Miracle of Theism*, Oxford University Press, Oxford, 1982, pp. 13-29.
16   J. L. Mackie, "The Relevance Criterion of Confirmation", *British Journal for the Philosophy of Science*, 1969, 20, pp. 27-40. More concisely, the principle is $P(H|E) > P(H)$ if and only if $P(E|H) > P(E)$. This discussion is about the philosophical principles concerning evidence as support for hypotheses; it does not address the biblical issue of whether miracles were meant to provide evidence for the supernatural (see 'Addendum', following).

3.
Miracles as evidence for Christianity

Archie Poulos

ARGUMENTS ABOUT MIRACLES have historically formed a large part of debate about the truth of Christianity. Hume's arguments are still discussed as part of the basic syllabus in university philosophy courses and are quoted as reason not to accept the reliability of Christianity's historical accounts. It is a sad reflection on the proponents of this tradition that it survives, and that the arguments ever convinced Hume (not to mention his followers since). For even if the arguments were philosophically valid, they fail to impinge upon the truth of Christianity, for they are based on ideas that fail to take the Bible on its own terms. A very cursory glance at the New Testament demonstrates that the Bible does not argue for what Hume considers he disproved. Miracles are not presented in the New Testament as proof of the truth of Christian doctrine, nor even of the existence of the supernatural; on the contrary, Jesus Christ himself threw doubt upon miracles as a basis of faith. That is, the assumption that in Christianity miracles are meant to authenticate or create faith is quite wrong, according to the Christian documents themselves.

This can be seen at several places in the New Testament, but a few examples suffice to demonstrate the point. For instance, consider the parable told by Jesus in Luke 16 about the rich man and the beggar, Lazarus. The rich man who in the afterlife is in torment, calls to Abraham to send Lazarus back to the rich man's brothers to warn them so that they might not meet the same fate. Abraham's reply to the rich man in the parable is instructive: "If they do not listen to Moses and the Prophets, they will not be convinced even if someone rises from the dead". The analogy with the miracle of Jesus' own resurrection is quite plain. Even if seen face-to-face, those who wish to deny it will not be convinced.

A similar reaction occurred even among Jesus' own disciples, who could be said (and have been said by those arguing against Christianity) to be predisposed to believe. As described in Luke 24:36-49, they were confronted with the risen Jesus, touched him and saw him eat, but still did not really believe what they were seeing until Jesus explained the meaning of his resurrection from the Old Testament. Without the background information to make sense of the astounding event before them, they could hardly credit what they were seeing. Even those expected to be most prone to wishful thinking were more inclined to doubt the evidence before them than to accept that such a counterintuitive event could have taken place. A similar event is reported in Matthew 28:17: "When they saw him, they worshipped him; but some doubted".

As well as these occasions in which it is not expected that a miracle would convince those who did not understand the significance of the event, there are examples in the New Testament of people who do believe on account of miracles, but who are hardly presented in a positive light. For instance, we have the intriguing words of John 2:23-24: "Now while he [Jesus] was in Jerusalem at the Passover Feast, many people saw the miraculous signs he was doing and believed his name. But Jesus would not entrust himself to them, for he knew all men." Those who believed because of a display of supernatural power were not necessarily trustworthy; they may have been merely credulous, or impressed by the sensational with no depth of understanding. In fact in 2 Thessalonians 2:9 the "lawless one" who is doing the work of Satan is able to perform miracles, signs and wonders—an indication that the miraculous is no guarantee of the presence of God. (Compare also the warning in Mark 13:22-23: "For false Christs and false prophets will appear and perform signs and miracles to deceive the elect—if that were possible. So be on your guard.")

In the New Testament, miracles are not presented as the authentication of the truth of the message, nor as a good basis for faith. Spectacular supernatural displays of power could even be the work of the enemy of God and simple credulity is never encouraged. Like all other events in the Bible, miracles on their own are taken to be dumb. Without proper context and explanation, they prove nothing either way. The miracles of Jesus are only taken as significant in the context of Old Testament prophecy, which gives the background understanding to explain the miracles as the work of the promised Messiah. Without the background knowledge, miracles are presented as dubious sources for faith at best. The only sense in which they provide some sort of ratification of Christian doctrines is when they are fully explained in the context of Old Testament theology. Without this interpretation, the human who sees the miracle is not expected to have grounds for believing that the doctrines of Christianity are true.

This helps to explain why at times the Bible *appears* to advocate belief on the basis of miracles. "Believe me when I say that I am in the Father and the Father is in me", says Jesus in John 14:11, "or at least believe on the evidence of the miracles themselves". A similar Old Testament passage is found in Isaiah 42-48, where God points to his works as proof that he is the only God and protector of his people. Such passages must not be misread to contradict what has been said above. In each of these incidents, the miracle is given an explanation which provides the reason for belief; the miracle does not stand alone. The parting of the Red Sea is explained as God's action in looking after his people, and Jesus' miracles as the work of the Father. Jesus also states that the disciples should believe because they trust his word; but if that is not enough, they have the miracles, which now have his word in explanation. In each case the word is the authentication of the miracle, not the other way around. Moreover, *what* people are to believe in both of these cases is not that the supernatural is real; rather, the objects of belief are particular pieces of information—that there is only one God, and that Jesus identifies himself with the Father.

It is worth adding a comment on another general misunderstanding of biblical miracles. That is, miracles in the Bible are not always presented as necessarily violating natural laws or being without secondary causes. For example, the miracle of the parting of the Red Sea is said in Exodus 14:21 to have been accomplished "with a strong east wind". While this event was certainly very unusual, it involved natural elements; the real miracle was in the purpose and timing of the event. The Bible does not present God as outside and remote from the world, with miracles as evidence of supernatural intervention. The biblical picture is of a God who controls all natural forces; a miracle, then, is a particularly significant act of God, not a particularly supernatural one. Indeed, in the Bible the very natural/supernatural distinction on which Hume based his argument is overturned. The 'supernatural' event is accomplished by natural means.

It was not unusual for Christian apologists of the seventeenth and eighteenth centuries to be concerned with demonstrating the truth of Christianity by appealing to the historicity of Jesus' miracles and resurrection. Hume was opposing a type of argument with which he was no doubt familiar; but whether or not he realised it, in doing so he was not opposing New Testament Christianity, merely its seventeenth-century apologists. While the debate is interesting, and it is worthwhile demonstrating the flaws in Hume's arguments, we should also realise that those arguments were in any case based on a false impression of Christianity.

4.
Giordano Bruno: enigmatic martyr

Kirsten Birkett

W HO WAS GIORDANO Bruno? During his lifetime
in the late sixteenth century, he was a controversial figure of some fame in England, France and Italy. After his
death, his fame continued; vilified in seventeenth-century writing, by the nineteenth century he was the
champion of free thought. Although the name leaves
most people looking blank now, in 1926 a bibliography
compiled of works about Bruno numbered around
2,000 items. In certain historical disciplines he is still
very well-known; and in more popular literature, in
particular the literature about the relationship between
science and religion, mention of him is becoming gradually more common.

For instance, when *New Scientist* published 'The
Complete Scientific History of the Universe', it portrayed as one of the 'persecutions' of science (symbol-
ised with a cross) "1600: Giardano Bruno [sic] burnt at
the stake for supporting the Copernican theory and
other heresies".[1] Cosmologist Paul Davies is another
who has recently cited Bruno as a martyr to science:

"Indeed, the 16th-century philosopher, Giordano Bruno, was burnt at the stake for insisting that we are not alone in the universe—a view that collided with the doctrine of the Catholic Church".[2]

Who was this man who has commanded so much attention, and such varied judgements, for some four hundred years? He was a runaway Dominican monk, a philosopher, a religious reformer and prolific writer who was executed at the age of 52. His philosophy was at considerable odds with his contemporaries. Amongst other things, he agreed with Copernicus that the earth moved. He also suggested that the stars were themselves like suns, and may well have inhabited worlds circling them. He shattered the small medieval universe, pushing its boundaries out to infinity. However his beliefs were too much for the Roman church authorities: after a brief lifetime of some fame in several European countries, he was imprisoned in Rome and eventually executed for heresy.

A study of Giordano Bruno takes the researcher into some surprising areas. He appears in such diverse fields as Christopher Marlowe's drama, Stuart theatre, and James Joyce's prose.[3] He wrote poetry, comedy, and theories of occult magic as well as philosophy. He appears in the records of Geneva, Paris, Elizabethan England, Wittenberg, Venice and finally Rome—the only place where he was not able to escape the hostility created by his outspoken views. He moved in powerful company, with private audiences to teach the French king, and living with the French ambassador in London;

he was a frequent visitor to Elizabeth's court, and also took part in learned debate in the leading universities of Europe. It even appears now likely that he was a spy on behalf of Elizabeth, selling secrets of the French ambassador who was involved in an intrigue to rescue the Catholic Mary Queen of Scots.[4]

Giordano Bruno was burnt alive at the stake. It was a horrible death, the thought of which should make any reader shudder. In an age of brutal punishments for crime, Bruno was unfortunate enough to suffer a terrible penalty. If we are discussing the topic of brutal death, Bruno—like millions of others in the history of humanity, in countless horrible ways—counts as one who suffered terribly. As we condemn brutality in any circumstance, so we condemn this.

But what beliefs? This is the topic of this article, for Bruno is not held up simply as a martyr of humanity in a sinful world, but in particular as a martyr for science against an oppressive religion. It is held that Bruno died because of his adherence to Copernicanism and his belief in the infinity of the universe. Bruno, like Galileo, is quoted as an example of the way in which historical religion has squashed scientific progress, in this case with the execution of a free-thinking man who committed no other crime than to believe the truth in advance of his contemporaries. In an effort to understand history correctly, and to gain a somewhat more accurate picture of who Giordano Bruno was and what happened to him, we will try to trace some of his life and thought. The aim is to avoid misusing an historical figure; in order to ensure that, we need a better under-standing of history.

Giordano Bruno is in many ways a confusing man to study, and a lot of information about him has been lost. What is more, many of the surviving documents remain untranslated into English. However the English studies of Bruno's work go into considerable detail, and this essay aims to demonstrate that even in this easily available literature a corrective to the public myth is available. In the case of Bruno, like Galileo, the reading public is in danger of being presented with a caricature that has very little to do with real history. In an effort to prevent a legend as inaccurate as Galileo's from entering public consciousness, let us see what is known about this complex character.[5]

The life of Giordano Bruno

Most of what we know of Bruno's history comes from the records of his interrogation before the Inquisition in Venice, with some corroboration and detail from places he visited. Bruno was born at Nola, a small town on the foothills of Vesuvius, in 1548. He entered the Dominican Order in Naples, and was given the monastic name of Giordano which he kept for the rest of his life. He began an education fairly normal for the time, Aristotelian and scholastic. While still young he began to develop a system of improving the memory, and around 1571, when only 23, he was apparently summoned to Rome to expound his system. However by his late twenties he was in trouble, and he twice had proceedings against him, once for throwing away images of the saints, once for recommending a novice to read a certain book. In 1576 a report began to circulate that he supported the Arian heresy, and he learned that an indictment was being prepared against him in Naples; he fled, abandoning his Dominican habit.

Bruno's first place of refuge was the tiny town of Noli in Genoese territory, where he taught astronomy and grammar. Passing through Venice, he made his way to Padua where some fellow Dominicans persuaded him to resume his habit. In time he did so, but in 1579 reached Calvinist Geneva and finally renounced his Dominican allegiance. Later at his trial in Venice Bruno stated that despite his journeys in Protestant lands, he had never intended to adopt Protestantism; this was most likely true, not just a pious fiction to please his captors, for Bruno constantly held himself indifferent to and above the quarrels between Catholic and Protestant. However he managed to alienate his Protestant hosts fairly quickly by publishing a violent attack on the professor of philosophy at the Genevan University. Bruno apologised, but took the opportunity of his public apology to protest that the ministers of the Geneva Church were mere pedagogues and did not understand his writings. He was not expelled from the city, but it had become uncomfortable for him, so he turned to France.

Bruno arrived in Paris in 1581. He gave public lectures, wrote a play, and published books on the art of memory which make use of natural magic—although how much he intended as magical incantation, and how much was merely allegory rich in symbolism, is a matter of debate.[6] The Roman orators had used mnemonics (aids to memory) for their practised speeches, memorising a series of places in a building and attaching images which would remind them of points of their speech. This was purely a technical way of memorising a speech. Bruno used a similar technique, but with magical or mystical images rather than an imaginary building: the decans (zodiacal gods), the planets and the houses of the horoscope. His second book on memory, *Cantus Circaeus*, was more strongly magical. It contained incantations based on *De occulta philosophia* of Cornelius Agrippa.[7]

Certainly King Henri III of France was interested in the technique, whether magical or natural. Bruno met Henri III in Paris, and it appears he was well-received. Later events seem to indicate that he had some protection from the French king, although Bruno denied to his inquisitors that he was teaching Henri magic. For instance, Bruno claimed he had letters of introduction from the French king to the French ambassador in England. This indeed may have been true, for the French ambassador gave considerable protection to Bruno during his stay in England.

Bruno arrived in England in 1583, and in the two years he was to spend there he produced his most significant cosmological works. His reputation went before him: the English ambassador in Paris had already written to Francis Walsingham of "Doctor Jordan

Bruno Nolano, a professor in philosophy...whose religion I cannot commend".[8] While in England, Bruno offended the Oxford community, but experienced a much celebrated notoriety amongst the London elite. The story of how Oxford came to reject him is interesting in itself, and provides some insight into Bruno's character.

Sometime in 1583, Bruno went to Oxford.[9] That year, a nobleman from the Continent, Prince Albert Laski, was visiting England and Queen Elizabeth requested that Oxford arrange for his entertainment. Accordingly, the Oxford dons arranged debates, lectures and other intellectual displays. Apparently Bruno travelled to Oxford with the Prince, and so was present for these festivities. It also seems that one of the entertainments arranged was a debate between Bruno and an Oxford scholar, Dr John Underhill. We do not know the topic of this debate, but a note from a member of the audience records that Bruno "went on to argue most readily about every conceivable matter."[10] Bruno himself recalled this debate with some vehemence. He claimed that he answered all arguments most learnedly, and that the "poor doctor" who was arguing against him "felt like a chick on a leash". He also referred to the "uncouthness and discourtesy" with which "that pig" (his Oxford opponent) acted, contrasting it with his own "extraordinary patience and humanity".[11]

During another visit to Oxford to give a lecture series, Bruno apparently defended the Copernican hypothesis, among other things.[12] George Abbot, later

Archbishop of Canterbury but then master of University College, referred to this lecture series with some contempt. He made fun of Bruno's peculiar (to Oxford ears) pronunciation of Latin terms, and derided him as someone who "more boldly than wisely" tried to defend the Copernican system. Abbot was not impressed: "he undertooke among very many other matters to set on foote the opinion of Copernicus, that the earth did goe round, and the heavens did stand still; wheras in truth it was his owne head which rather did run round, and his braines did not stand stil."[13] Moreover, Bruno was accused of plagiarism, Abbott wrote: one of the audience found two of Bruno's lectures "taken almost verbatim out of the workes of Marsilius Ficinus".[14] This is a peculiar reference, for Marsilius Ficinus wrote of Hermetic magic, and based his astrological system on a thoroughly traditional earth-centred universe. It is hard to see how lectures defending Copernicus could have been taken verbatim from Ficinus. However it was this evidence which led scholar Francis Yates to posit that Bruno's adherence to Copernican theory, in general terms at least, was closely linked with his schemes for magical reformation.[15]

In any case, Bruno left considerable bad feeling behind him in Oxford. He returned to London and wrote about Copernicanism in the dialogue *La cena de le ceneri*, 'The Ash-Wednesday Supper', in which his bitter words above about Oxford are found. He followed this dialogue with other works in Italian which describe his far-reaching cosmology with magical or pantheistic undertones. In one of these, *Spaccio de la bestia trionfante*, 'The Expulsion of the Trimphant Beast', an allegory telling the story of a reform of heaven by Jupiter, Bruno praised the ancient Egyptian religion as more pure than the later Christianity, which was a corruption of the ancient wisdom.[16]

At the end of 1585 Bruno's patron, the French ambassador, was recalled to Paris. Bruno went with him, and re-entered Parisian intellectual society. Bruno approached various church officials for absolution and admission to the Mass, but was told he must first return to his order, which he refused to do. He continued writing on his system of memory, as well as philosophy. At the same time he decided to defend one Fabrizio Mordente who had invented the eight-pointed compass, and whom Bruno thought had not received sufficient credit for it. Unfortunately Bruno chose to describe Mordente as an ass, and a triumphant idiot, who did not fully understand his own invention.[17] Mordente was enraged, and went to the authorities for support against Bruno. Bruno also, while in Paris, set up a public debate where he claimed he would defend one hundred and twenty articles of nature against the Aristotelians. The debate apparently attracted quite a large audience, and Bruno's anti-Aristotelian claims were read out by one of his pupils. These were answered by a young scholar. Bruno surprisingly left the debate at that point without reply, but with the promise he would return the next day for further argument. Apparently he did not, but was soon known to be gone from the city. It is probably significant that the young scholar who had opposed Bruno was from King Henri's circle; Bruno could no longer count on royal support.[18] In any case, Paris was in political turmoil, soon to be thrown into war, and it was no place of safety for a controversial scholar.

Bruno's next stay was in Germany, returning once more to Protestant territory. He first went to Marburg to study at the university there, but his fiery nature brought his study to an abrupt end. When he was not given permission to teach philosophy he "impudently reviled" the University Rector (according to the Rector) and declared he had no wish to remain a member of the Academy.[19] Bruno then went to Wittenburg, where he stayed for two years, as a university teacher. Bruno was in admiration of the Lutherans; he later told the Venetian Inquisitors that he only left because a Calvinist party became more powerful there. Early in 1588 Bruno left for Prague, where the Emperor Rudoph II was gathering astrologers and alchemists to assist him in his search for the philosopher's stone. From there Bruno went to Helmstedt, where he was excommunicated by a Protestant pastor, but also received favour from the young Duke Henry Julius;[20] with money received from the Duke, Bruno published six Latin poems which further explored his mystical cosmology. Finally, after a brief stay with one Hainzell or Heinz who entertained those with a reputation for alchemy and occultism, Bruno took the step that led to his downfall. He returned to Italy.

Bruno's trial

Bruno's life already reveals him as a strange controversialist. His life was certainly unusual for a sixteenth-century scholar, and just settling the details of what happened during his vagabond lifetime has presented ample scope for scholarly discussion. However his travels are overshadowed by the question of the end of his life. How was it that Bruno ended up on the stake in 1600, sentenced to death? What precisely was he charged with, and what was his defence? We might start with the question of why Bruno returned to Italy at all, knowing that he had fled religious charges in the first place. Commentators speculate that this return is indicative of Bruno's supreme indifference to religious arguments, and an almost unworldly naivety in his presumption that he would not be in danger.[21] It has also been argued that Bruno, always deeply interested in magic, planned to enchant Pope Clement VIII.[22] Even without the magic, there is indication that he hoped that Italy would be invaded by Henri of Navarre, the theologically liberal clamaint to the French throne.[23] Whatever the case, the immediate cause of his return to Italy was an offer of employment.

It was a Venetian of noble birth, Zuane Mocenigo, who invited Bruno to Italy. He wished to be taught Bruno's art of memory. Bruno lodged in Mocenigo's house, but when he informed Mocenigo of a desire to return to Frankfurt to get certain of his works printed, Mocenigo was apparently filled with a jealous fear that Bruno would impart his secrets to others, and threatened him with the Inquisition. When Bruno insisted on leaving, Mocenigo imprisoned Bruno, still demanding to be taught the secrets of memory. Bruno was tried by the Inquisition at Venice, and it is from the records of this trial that we have most of his history. Bruno was examined in great length on points of doctrine, especially on the Trinity. He pleaded that certain heretical passages in his works were not in defiance of the Catholic faith, but were merely philosophical discussion, or deliberate listing of the beliefs of heretics. He was also questioned concerning his praise for Queen Elizabeth and other heretical persons. Bruno wished to placate his examiners, and openly recanted anything that may be held to be non-Catholic.[24]

In September of 1592, letters arrived from Rome demanding that Bruno be sent there to stand trial. The Venice Office of the Inquisition was not at all quick to hand him over, resenting the incursion upon Venetian independence; but eventually in February 1593 Bruno went to Rome.

Of the longer trial at Rome little record remains. In 1810 part of the Roman archives were taken to Paris on the orders of Napoleon whose intention was to centralise the secret archives of all Europe. The treaties of 1815 stipulated that such documents should be restored to their countries of origin, but while on their return journey the documents relating to Bruno's trial disappeared. A summary of the trial was discovered in 1940 and published in 1942. There is also certain evidence from contemporaries.[25] From these sparse records, it is possible to determine that while in prison before his trial Bruno was questioned on the matter of heresy. A fellow-prisoner reported him for saying that the cross on Christian altars was in reality the sign of the goddess Isis, stolen by the Christians from the Egyptians. He defended magic, saying that those who knew the virtues of the stars, and how to use images and characters, could use such magic for good.[26]

In 1599 eight heretical propositions were drawn up which Bruno was required to abjure, and he said he was prepared to do so. Later in that year, however, he withdrew all his retractions and maintained that he had never written or said anything heretical. Unfortunately the report of the eight heretical propositions which Bruno was required to recant has been lost, so there is no record of precisely what he was accused of. There is however a surviving summary of a reply by "Frater Jordanus" to censures on propositions drawn from his works, which may indicate what the censures were. It touches on ideas of the infinite universe and the motion of the earth amongst many other things. A witness to the death of Bruno who may have heard the sentence read out gives a mixed list of points: that Bruno denied transubstantiation; that his work *Spaccio* was held to refer to the Pope as the "Triumphant Beast"; that he taught "horrible absurdities" such as infinite worlds, the transmigration of souls, the lawfulness of magic, that the Holy Spirit is the *anima mundi*; that Moses did his miracles by magic in which he was more proficient than the Egyptians; and that Christ was a magus.[27]

However, the trial documents being lost, there is no definite record of what Bruno was charged with. The only indication that his 'scientific' views had anything to do with his trial comes from the vague document mentioned above, which is not definitely connected with Bruno's condemnation. The evidence indicates that Bruno's theological views were far more serious crimes. What is known of Bruno's religious views certainly put him within the Catholic category of 'heretic'. One recent biographer says he "despised and detested Jesus, and had a special contempt for the Cross and for any form of the mass or the eucharist".[28] Bruno's final sentence accused him of heresy, and he was delivered to the Secular Court for punishment. The execution was on 17 Feb 1600.[29]

Bruno and Copernicanism

Did Bruno defend Copernicus; and if he did, why? Answering these questions is more complicated than it might seem, partly because Bruno wrote in such a highly polemical and frequently allegorical style. Bruno several times referred to Copernicus, but his main discussion of Copernicus' work was in the dialogue entitled *La Cena de la Ceneri*, 'The Ash Wednesday Supper'. The dialogue is in the form of a debate about cosmology between Bruno and two Oxford scholars, set in London. There may indeed have been such a debate; or this may merely be Bruno's idealised answer to the scorn he evoked when he was in Oxford. The strangest thing about this dia-

logue in defence of Copernicus is what a poor account
Bruno gave of Copernicus' theory. He seems to have
misunderstood some of its basic tenets.

For instance, at one point in the dialogue the
Oxonian, Torquato, was ridiculed for misunderstanding Copernicus. Torquato thought that the earth was
the third planet from the sun, with the moon revolving
around it. But "even the greatest ass in the world",
replied Bruno's character, knew that Copernicus said
something quite different; the earth and the moon
both revolved around a point which itself revolved
around the sun. Torquato, said Bruno, had misunderstood Copernicus' diagram; what he thought was the
earth "was only the mark of the compass left when
drawing the epicycle of the earth and the moon."[30] In
fact Torquato was quite right. Copernicus had made it
clear that the earth, the third planet revolving around
the sun, was the centre of the moon's orbit; Bruno had
simply misunderstood. Later in the dialogue other con-
fusions about Copernicus' theory arose.[31]

In another work, Bruno proposed a model of the
planetary system which was different again; and this
time not only at odds with Copernicus, but with the
accumulated body of astronomical observations. He
claimed that Venus and Mercury were on a single
epicycle, at the same distance from the sun as an earth-
moon epicycle, but on the opposite side from the Sun.
Bruno's own system, then, had neither mathematical
simplicity nor observational evidence in support of it.[32]
In fact, Bruno was generally disdainful of astronomers

and their mathematical reasoning.[33] Ptolemy and Copernicus both, he said, had reported what they understood well enough, but what they understood was not much; they were like the peasants who reported to the captain. The captain (Bruno himself) was the one with the understanding to make sense of what they had written.[34]

The second, and probably more interesting, question is, what were Bruno's reasons for embracing a new cosmology? This has caused a great deal of debate. Frances Yates claimed that Bruno saw the Copernican system as a magical hieroglyph or symbol; that he was not persuaded of its truth by physical or mathematical reasoning, but that he could see a hidden meaning beyond the mere theory. Yates has been criticised for taking this view too far,[35] but certainly Bruno's approach to Copernicanism was far from what we would label 'scientific'. For instance, his argument against the Aristotelian dependence on circular orbits for the planets was not mathematical, but because planets, as living beings, determine their own orbits. He saw the planets as alive, and with souls. The cause of the local motion of the earth was renewal and rebirth, as in other living things. The stars are not only alive, but are in some sense deities, and "keep their proper distances in order to participate in perpetual life." The planets circle the sun in order to communicate with one another.[36]

In fact, Bruno's excitement about Copernicus was largely because his radical break with old astronomy heralded a new age in which the ancient philosophy would now be seen to be true. This ancient philosophy was that of the Chaldeans, the Egyptians, the magi, the Orphists and of the Pythagoreans: that is, a mystical and religious understanding of nature. Misguided logicians and mathematicians had done humanity a disservice in moving away from this ancient knowledge. However now the light was breaking through, and Bruno was announcing the truth once more: that there are living principles in all things, the sun, stars and soul participate in divinity and so on. The earth must move, not for mathematical reasons, but so it may renew itself and be born again.[37] Bruno's criticisms of Copernicus have led one commentator to say that "To call Bruno a 'Copernican' requires one to empty the label of all content save the assertion that the earth and planets move around the sun. Not only does his arrangement of the planets differed entirely from that of Copernicus, as we have seen, but he separates himself in the most emphatic way from the methodology on which Copernicus rests his case".[38]

It is hardly accurate to claim that Bruno presaged modern science. He was certainly capable of detailed philosophical argument, and many of his criticisms of Aristotle (for instance) indicate a superb philosophical mind. He was in many ways a brilliant thinker, but always an eccentric one. His mystical views, while they led him to certain familiar ideas—the movement of the earth, and the existence of other planets—were far from the conclusions of modern cosmology.

Bruno and history

What can we conclude from this story? What we know of Bruno is a rather fragmented and confusing portrait of a very strange man. His writings are difficult to read, and that they are difficult to understand is testified to by the amount of discussion over what he actually meant.[39] He is an enigmatic figure, highly idiosyncratic, who can hardly be held as a figurehead for any particular philosophical view except his own. He was a controversialist who insulted almost every religious and political camp of Europe. Those who make Bruno the martyr of science are very selective in what they remember about him. He is hailed as a hero because of his Copernicanism—in name at least—but his hermetic magic and religious writings are conveniently ignored. Even so, Bruno's peculiar version of Copernicanism, while interesting, was hardly a step towards modern science; and it was not the reason for his martyrdom.

This is a fairly simple point to make. Why is it then that Bruno is still quoted as a scientific martyr? Even on the most generalised of historical readings, it is not true. Yet the survival of this kind of glib 'proof-text' of the church's supposed antipathy to science signals something quite apart from a rational concern for truth. The science–religion 'war' will not die. It is still just too convenient a metaphor for an anti-Christian bias, and it persists no matter how many times the inaccuracy of its individual statements is demonstrated. It seems rather ironic that even where Galileo's story is well-known, another martyr is quoted with even more inaccuracy.

If nothing else, this article is simply a call for a little more care in science writing. It matters to a great many people what the real relationship is between science and religion, and whatever one's position in that discussion, at least the issues should be portrayed accurately. There is no need to distort history, and the discussion is hardly helped forward from anyone's point of view if such carelessness is fostered. It is a small matter to correct a common misunderstanding about Bruno, but it is part of redirecting a larger discussion.

ENDNOTES

1   It is notable that this article also included such historically dubious sentiments as "If it hadn't been for the rise of Christianity and the destruction of classical thought, could we have reached this point in our scientific evolution a thousand years earlier?" and "412: the murder of Hypatia by a Christan mob in Alexandria signals the end of 'pagan' science and its replacement by religious dogma". *New Scientist*, 28 October 1995, pp. 26-29.

2   *The Sydney Morning Herald*, August 10, 1996, p. 27.

3   Hilary Gatti, 'Giordano Bruno and the Stuart Court Masques', *Renaissance Quarterly*, 1995, *48*, pp. 809-42; Roy T. Eriksen, 'Giordano Bruno and Marlowe's *Doctor Faustus*', *Notes and Queries*, 1985, *32*, pp. 464-5; and Gino Moliterno, 'The Candlebearer at the *Wake*: Bruno's *Candelaio* in Joyce's Book of the Dark', *Comparative Literature Studies*, 1993, *30*, pp. 269-93.

4   John Bossy, *Giordano Bruno and the Embassy Affair*, Yale University Press, New Haven and London, 1991.

5   As already indicated, a great deal has been written about Bruno, a large part of it not in English. For English studies, see Dorothea Waley Singer, *Giordano Bruno: His Life and Thought*, Greenwood Press, New York, 1968; Frances A. Yates, *Giordano Bruno and the Hermetic Tradition*, The University of Chicago Press, Chicago and London, 1964; Paul Henri Michel, *The Cosmology of Giordano Bruno*, trans. R. E. W. Maddison, Hermann, Paris, 1973.

Bossy *op. cit.*, has a good general biography of manuscript and published sources concerning Bruno. For studies of more particular aspects of Bruno's life and philosophy, see Hilary Gatti, *The Renaissance Drama of Knowledge: Giordano Bruno in England*, Routledge, London and New York, 1989; Frances A. Yates, *The Art of Memory*, Pimlico, London, 1966 and *Lull and Bruno: Collected Essays*, Routledge and Kegan Paul, London, 1982. This account is based on the English works mentioned above; I have not read the trial documents which appear to be published only in Italian. For English translations of Bruno's cosmological works, see *The Ash Wednesday Supper*, Edward Gosselin and Lawrence Lerner (eds and trans.), University of Toronto Press, Toronto, 1995; *The Expulsion of the Triumphant Beast*, Arthur D. Imerti (trans. and ed.), Rutgers University Press, New Brunswick, 1964; 'On the Infinite Universe and Worlds', appendix to Singer's book, *op. cit.*; and *Cause, Principle and Unity*, Jack Lindsay (trans.), Background Books, Essex, 1962.

6   Singer, for instance, tends to downplay the magical elements; *op. cit.*, p. 18.

7   Yates, *op. cit.*, pp. 199-202.

8   Quoted in Yates *op. cit.*, p. 204.

9   See Ernan McMullin, 'Giordano Bruno at Oxford', *Isis*, 1986, 77, pp. 85-94.

10   *Ibid.*, p. 85, quoting a marginal note of Gabriel Harvey.

11   *The Ash Wednesday Supper*, Gosselin and Lerner *op. cit.*, p. 187.

12   McMullin, *op. cit.*, p. 86.

13   Yates, *op. cit.*, p. 208.

14   *Ibid*; McMullin *op. cit.*, p. 93.

15   See for instance Yates, *Giordano Bruno, op. Cit.*, ch.12.

16   This work was mentioned by name during Bruno's trial; see Singer, *op. cit.*, p. 176.

17   Yates *op, cit.*, pp. 294-298..

18   *Ibid.*, pp. 299-302. The account of the debate is from the diary of a librarian who knew Bruno in Paris; the connection between the defender of Aristotle and King Henri III is Yates' speculation.

19   Singer, *op. cit.*, p. 139, quoting the record of the event written by the offended Rector.

20   *Ibid.*, p. 146. It is not known why Bruno was excommuni-

cated, and furthermore it is curious that Bruno could be excommunicated as there is no record of him ever formally joining the Protestants. As Singer says, the matter is somewhat obscure.

21 For instance, McIntyre suggests that Bruno probably did not realise he was in danger, or what sort of reputation he had. J. Lewis McIntyre, *Giordano Bruno*, Macmillan and Co, London, 1903, pp. 69, 70. Singer wrote of Bruno's character in a different context, "Bruno was in his incurable mental detachment in fact completely indifferent to the quarrels between Catholic and Protestant, regarding them as irrelevant to the high philosophic problems that occupied his mind to the exclusion of all worldly wisdom and even of the commonest prudence", *op. cit.*, pp. 14-15.

22 Bossy, *op. cit.*, p. 154.

23 *Ibid.*, p. 155, citing Mocenigo's testimony to the Inquisition.

24 Singer, *op. cit.*, pp. 158−168.

25 See Michel, *op. cit.*, p. 18.

26 Yates, *op. cit.*, pp. 351, 353.

27 Quoted in *ibid.*, p. 354; also McIntyre, p. 93.

28 Bossy, *op. cit.*, p. 148.

29 McIntyre suggests that even Bruno's published heresies were not enough grounds for his sentence, but that his theological views were so radical he was regarded as the founder of a new religion and so especially dangerous. *Op. cit.*, p. 98.

30 'The Ash Wednesday Supper', Gosselin and Lerner, *op. cit.*, p. 192. These mistakes of Bruno's were identified by Ernan McMullin, 'Bruno and Copernicus', *Isis*, 1987, *78*, pp. 55-74.

31 *Ibid.*, p. 57.

32 *Ibid.*, p. 59, discussing Bruno's *De immenso*.

33 Robert S. Westman writes "Needless to say, Bruno's disdain for mathematics has led to mixed judgements among scholars. How can one reconcile Bruno's brilliant physical intuitions with his frequently shocking mathematical reasoning?". His suggested answer is that for all his attacks on Aristotle, Bruno was still influenced by Aristotle's denigration of mathematics, and was probably very ill-trained in mathematics himself. 'Magical reform and astronomical reform: the Yates thesis reconsidered', in pp. 1-91 in Robert S. Westman and J. E. McGuire (eds), *Hermeticism and the Scientific Revolution*, William Andrews Clark

Memorial Library, Los Angeles, 1977, pp. 1-91, p. 34.

34 McMullin, 'Bruno and Copernicus', *op. cit.*, p. 60.

35 Westman *op. cit.*, argued that while Yates "has greatly enriched our understanding of Bruno by protraying him as a religio-political prophet and would-be Hermetic reformer" (p. 13), Hermeticism should not be over-stated as the only motivator for Bruno's thought. Westman instead sees the key in Bruno's theology; the infinite cause, God, must create an infinite effect, which is animated by the infinite world soul (p. 30).

36 McMullin, 'Bruno and Copernicus', *op. cit.*, pp. 61-62, taking ideas from 'The Ash Wednesday Supper', *op. cit.*, pp. 156, 213, 91, 185.

37 McMullin, *ibid.*, p. 65; 'The Ash Wednesday Supper', *Ibid.*, pp. 94-95.

38 McMullin, *ibid.*, p. 64.

39 Views about Bruno are almost as confusing as Bruno's work itself. Consider for instance the range of religious admirers of Bruno, taken from Singer's chapter 'Influence of Bruno': John Toland, the eighteenth-century deist, warmly defended Bruno; the *Spectator* of 1712 described Bruno as 'a professed atheist'; F. H. Jacobi in 1789 claimed he could not understand why Bruno's philosophy was called obscure, as there was hardly a purer exposition of pantheism. To provide further contrast, a translator of Bruno's work this century insists that materialist dialectic must be recognised as the core of Bruno (Jack Lindsay, preface to his translation of *Cause, Principle and Unity*, Background Books, Essex, 1962).

5.
Darwin and the fundamentalists
Kirsten Birkett

"The theory of evolution by natural selection is seriously discredited in the biological world."
Vernon L. Kellog, leading biologist[1]

"[I am] a Darwinian of the purest water."
B. B. Warfield, fundamentalist theologian[2]

READERS MIGHT BE forgiven for thinking that the names attached to the above quotations have been inadvertently switched around. Indeed, so surprising is it these days to consider that two men from their respective camps ever made such statements, somewhere along the line our understanding of history must have become severely distorted. It would never occur to most people that one of the founding fundamentalists could describe himself in this way—or that, at one point, he could find himself defending aspects of Darwinism against atheist biologists. It is worth our time, then, to examine what actually was the response of Bible-believing (and defending) Christian thinkers to Darwinian evolution during its early influence.

It is worth our time particularly because there is a popular perception that evolution has proved that Christianity is untrue. The legend might run like this: Darwin came along and the church fell, for there was no reason for God any more. The story usually includes mention of at least two 'crucial' battles. The first is the debate between Huxley and Wilberforce at Oxford in 1860. "Soapy Sam" Wilberforce, the stereotypical English clergyman, was defeated by the witty intelligence of the scientist Thomas Huxley, and the creaking institution of the church was pushed aside by the new man of science. Many years later, in 1925, the Scopes Trial turned the issue of whether evolution could be taught in American schools into national news. Those who held to biblical truth—the fundamentalists—became a national laughing stock, stripped of intellectual credibility. These two debates typify the stock picture of science-church relationships; the church coming out as weak and ineffectual, and ridiculously anti-intellectual.

Fundamentalists did indeed defend the Bible; but most people have very little idea of what this means. 'Fundamentalists' are caricatured as unthinking, unreflective dogmatists, and if they are the Bible's supporters, it is often concluded that the Bible is not worth defending. Many now use the word 'fundamentalism' as a generic term for anti-progressive dogmatism, knowing nothing of the actual movement in America which started with a series of books called *The Fundamentals*.[3] Most people do not realise, moreover, that the series was strongly influenced by one of the most respectable intellectual institutions in America at the time—Princeton Theological Seminary—and that the authors included internationally famous thinkers. The consequence of such ignorance of history is that, in today's intellectual atmosphere, to believe the Bible at all means being labelled 'fundamentalist', which automatically means anti-intellectual. Indeed, now that the word has become connected politically with the right-wing, sociologically with bigotry and reactionism, and has even been applied to militant terrorist branches of other religions, one need only say 'fundamentalist' to end any consideration of what such a person says. We have reached the point where believing the Bible is linked by association with the worst kind of anti-progressive anti-intellectualism. Religious discussion can be rejected by the modern intellectual without even being considered; it is simply labelled and rejected. However, this label is being applied with no understanding of history or of what the fundamentalist movement was created to protect.[4]

It is important, therefore, that the reality behind the label is understood; that the history is not allowed to be distorted along with the word. It is worthwhile to attempt to refresh our collective memory about what did happen when Darwin's theory became widely known, and how real theologians reacted. This essay simply presents a few counter-examples to the received view. We are going to look at three prominent theologians who wrote responses to Darwin in the decades following his theory. They were all Biblical defenders.

One was an immensely influential theologian in the Princeton tradition which shaped the religious life of America for nearly a century, and which stood firmly for Biblical authority. The other two, slightly later, were amongst the founding fathers of fundamentalism, as authors of *The Fundamentals*. Those committed to the Bible who reacted to Darwinism were not the blinkered philistines of modern caricatures. They were thoughtful commentators who saw the difference between scientific inquiry and naturalistic philosophy, and were quite prepared to listen to the available evidence. In studying what these commentators wrote, we are simply attempting to gain access to real history, without falling into the traps of polemic and propagandist caricatures.

The three men considered here were intellectual leaders in the late nineteenth and early twentieth century, two from America and one from Scotland. Charles Hodge (1797-1878) and B. B. Warfield (1851-1921) were professors of theology at Princeton university; James Orr (1844-1913) was a professor of apologetics and systematic theology in Glasgow. This essay is not a complete history of the origins of fundamentalism, nor can it give a complete study of the evolutionary thought of these men.[5] Certain writings have been selected to give a cross-section of their discussion of different aspects of evolutionary theory: its naturalism, its relationship to the interpretation of the early chapters of Genesis, its relationship to theological issues such as sin, and the scientific coherence of the theory itself.

Charles Hodge: Princeton Theologian

Charles Hodge was one of the major forces in the intellectual tradition that defended the Bible and promoted Biblical Christianity in America. Princeton Theological Seminary was among the most influential institutions in the United States from the time of its founding in 1812 until its reorganization in 1929.[6] During this time four professors of theology—Archibald Alexander, Charles Hodge, his son Archibald Alexander Hodge and Benjamin Breckinridge Warfield (see later in this essay)—built up a strong tradition of Biblical conservatism. Part of this tradition was an emphasis on the responsibilities of intellectual leaders in society, especially the responsibilities of those who provided leadership in spiritual and ethical matters. As one of the most influential of the Princeton theologians, Hodge began the fight against liberalism which his successors A. A. Hodge and B. B. Warfield were to take on more fully. What is more, he wrote one of the earlier theological responses to Darwinism, in a book which was immensely popular, and provided one of the few early critiques (whether Christian or not) which understood Darwin's theory in scientific terms and discussed its implications.

Hodge taught at Princeton from 1822 until his death. He was committed to the reliability of Scripture and was fiercely Calvinist. He was a polemicist who strongly resisted efforts to move away from a strict Biblical understanding of sin, salvation and Christian morality. He, as well as Warfield after him, believed that proper understanding of God and a thoroughly explored theology was necessary for society, and society tended to agree; intellectuals such as Hodge and Warfield, and theologians at other universities, were consulted and listened to on ethical and intellectual issues. Hodge was also very well-informed in different scientific fields. As a man of the nineteenth century, his thoroughly Baconian view of science pervaded his understanding of the relationship between science and religion. That is, he saw science as ideally the strict and rational exercise of induction from the facts, and no more. Therefore science should only accept what has been proved by the facts; but what has been thus proved should be taken seriously.

> Science is not the opinions of man, but knowledge; and specially, according to use, the ascertained truths concerning the facts and laws of nature. To say, therefore, that the Bible contradicts science is to say that it contradicts facts, is to say that it teaches error, and to say that it teaches error is to say it is not the Word of God. The proposition that the Bible must be interpreted by science is all but self-evident. Nature is as truly a revelation of God as the Bible, and we only interpret the Word of God by the Word of God when we interpret the Bible by science.[7]

In Hodge's opinion, it was ridiculous, not to mention blasphemous, to make the Bible say something false. This meant that to admit that one had been wrong when demonstrated to be wrong—such as when it had been demonstrated that the sun did not move around the earth—was plain common sense. This did not mean twisting the Bible to say something it clearly did not. There was a two-fold evil: on the one hand being too ready to adopt the opinions of scientific men and "forced and unnatural interpretations of the Bible"; and on the other hand refusing to admit the opinions of men of science to have any voice in the interpretation of Scripture.

> Let Christians calmly wait until facts are indu-
> bitably established, so established that they com-
> mand universal consent among competent men,
> and then they will find that the Bible accords
> with those facts. In the meantime, men must be
> allowed to ascertain and authenticate scientific
> facts in their own way, just as Galileo determined
> the true theory of the heavens.[8]

Hodge's book-length comment on evolutionary theory, entitled *What is Darwinism?*, was written in 1874, fifteen years after the publication of *The Origin of Species* and three years after *The Descent of Man*. Hodge entered the debate at a time when the scientific community in America was coming cautiously around to an accept-ance of evolution—though not necessarily utilising Darwin's particular theory of natural selection[9]—and a theological response was needed. Hodge, mindful of his responsibility to society, provided one.

The most basic questions for humanity, he began, concern its origin and place in the universe. The

Scriptural answer is creation by God, an assertion which rests on the authority of the word of God. It not only accounts for the origin of the universe, and everything the universe contains, especially the adaptation of organisms to surroundings; it is also not in conflict with any truth of reason or fact of experience, and it accounts for the spiritual nature of man. "The Bible has little charity for those who reject it. It pronounces them to be either derationalized or demoralized, or both."[10]

There had always been other theories to compete with the Biblical one: pantheism, epicureanism, and lately, Darwinism. Darwin, not a philosopher, did not speculate on the origin of the universe, or the nature of matter or such things; he was a skilful naturalist and a careful observer, and asked only the question, "How are the fauna and flora of our earth to be accounted for?" His answer was simple. All organisms descended from the one primordial germ, accounted for by the operation of the laws of heredity, variation, over-production and the law of natural selection or survival of the fittest.

The heart of Darwin's system, as Hodge saw it, lay in the word 'natural'. Darwin used the word in two ways; as antithetical to 'artificial' and also as antithetical to 'supernatural'. The point was, natural selection is done neither by man nor by a supernatural power. There is no design or higher cause. It is not an intelligent process, even though 'selection' is an active word.

Hodge elaborated upon this point. Darwinism, he said, includes three distinct elements: evolution (the assumption that all organic forms have developed from one or a few primordial living germs), natural selection, and the assertion that natural selection is without design. Now the first two of these, Hodge insisted, do not constitute Darwinism—a statement which would surprise us now, for modern definitions of Darwinism usually consist of "evolution by natural selection". Yet Hodge had his reasons. First of all, evolution was not equivalent to Darwinism because several scientists before Darwin taught that all species are descended from other species; and some evolutionists rejected Darwin's theory. Neither did natural selection mean Darwinism, for the concept of natural selection had appeared (though unrefined) in earlier theories of evolution.[11] What was distinctive about Darwinism was its rejection of teleology, or final causes.

This requires a little explanation. Teleology in nature is the idea that organisms have a final end toward which they aim; and that the development of the organism can be explained in terms of its final form. This doctrine is immediately appealing when we look at the natural world, and still dominates the way in which most people speak about nature. Why do birds have hollow bones? So that they are light enough to be able to fly. Why do plants have flowers? So they can germinate. This kind of explanation, which has been commonly accepted since ancient Greek times, has traditionally been seen to fit nicely with Christian theology. Since plants need to germinate, it made sense that God would make them with flowers; and the efficient functioning of the flowers was taken to be evidence of

God's wisdom in planning and designing nature.

Darwin, however, denied design, or the force of any intelligence or purpose behind the development of new organs and separate species. As Hodge put it,

> The point to be proved is that it is the distinctive doctrine of Mr. Darwin that species owe their origin, not to the original intention of the divine mind, not to special acts of creation calling new forms into existence at certain epochs, not to the constant and everywhere operative efficiency of God, guiding physical causes in the production of intended effects, but to the gradual accumulation of unintended variations of structure and instinct, securing some advantage to their subjects.[12]

It is interesting that Hodge had to go to some lengths to explain that Darwinism is ateleological. It was at that time not yet widely recognised how thoroughly Darwin's theory did away with final causes. Men who completely accepted teleology, Hodge stated, talked favourably of Darwinism in the same breath, not recognising the conflict. So Hodge spent page after page demonstrating from numerous examples from Darwin himself, from his supporters and from his critics—that his theory denies any end to which an organism is aiming.

At this point in his discussion, Hodge made a slight digression. Darwinism aside, he wished to discuss why it was that scientists and religious thinkers, as two classes, were so commonly perceived to be in conflict. It was not because science and religion were in conflict;

as we have seen, in Hodge's opinion the two could not be in conflict because both revealed truth. Yet it was evident that, however misplaced it might be in his view, there was an antagonism between scientists as a class and religious believers as a class. Why?

Firstly, Hodge pointed out that the two groups adopt different rules of evidence. Scientific 'knowledge' was restricted to the facts of nature or the external world. Science, in common usage, was the ordered knowledge of the phenomena which we recognize through the senses. This means that a conviction resting on any other ground was not science. "Darwin admits that the contrivances in nature may be accounted for by assuming that they are due to design on the part of God. But, he says, that would not be science."[13]

This was all very well; but it was illegitimate to assume that therefore the only valid convictions are those based on sense data. Yet sadly, Hodge said, scientists often let themselves fall into this very trap:

> It is inevitable that minds addicted to scientific investigation should receive a strong bias to undervalue any other kind of evidence except that of the senses....The tendency...of a mind addicted to the consideration of one kind of evidence to become more or less insensible to other kinds of proof is undeniable."[14]

As religion does not rest on the testimony of the senses, such people therefore ignore its evidence; even though the evidence is still there, and still just as reliable in its own sphere.

The second reason Hodge gives for why scientists fall into conflict with theologians was the failure to make the due distinction between *facts*, and the *explanation* of those facts or the theories deduced from them. Here Hodge again revealed his thoroughly Baconian view of science. Facts, in his view, were beyond question. They were revelation from God, 'pieces of truth' so to speak, and so Christians would and had changed their views when necessary before the facts (as they did when shown that the earth moved). However Hodge combined with this high opinion of fact a fairly cautious appraisal of human ability to infer correctly from fact. In other words, the willingness of Christians to change their views in face of the facts ought to satisfy scientific men, Hodge insisted; but instead, men of science want Christians to bow to their explanations and inferences too. "It is to be remembered that the facts are from God, the explanation from men; and the two are often as far apart as Heaven and its antipode."[15] The human explanations were not only without authority, but they were mutable. It is rather unreasonable, Hodge complained, that Christians are called upon to change their faith with every new scientific theory.

The third reason was a more sociological one; that is, conflict abides when scientists openly avow hostility to religion with an assumption of superiority and often a manifestation of contempt.

Professor Huxley's advice to metaphysicians and theologians is to let science alone...but do he and his associates let metaphysics and religion alone? They tell the metaphysician that his vocation is gone, there is no such thing as mind, and of course no mental laws to be established... Professor Huxley tells the religious world that there is overwhelming and crushing evidence (scientific evidence, of course) that no event has ever occurred on this earth which was not the effect of natural causes.

At the same time, the metaphysicians thus attacked were not allowed any right of reply. "If any protest be made against such doctrines, we are told that scientific truth cannot be put down by denunciation."[16]

What then was to be the outcome of the specific relationship between Darwinism and Christianity? Hodge found the theory itself unconvincing. He found it frankly incredible to suggest that all the plants and animals on earth came from one germ, especially by chance; "Taking all these things into consideration, we think it may with moderation be said that a more absolutely incredible theory was never propounded for acceptance among men."[17] This aside, there was no pretence even amongst the strongest Darwinists that the theory could be proved. All Darwin himself claimed of his theory was that it is possible. Hodge also noted that when the theory of evolution had been published in *Vestiges of the Natural History of Creation* twenty years before Darwin, it was universally rejected.[18] Twenty years later, however, it was received with acclamation. Why? Hodge thought it was because the *Vestiges* did not expressly or effectually exclude design. That is, evolution, banished in 1844, was popular in 1866 because it suited a prevailing state of mind. It suited those who wished to reject the supernatural from the world.

Hodge's third criticism of the theory was specifically scientific. He pointed out that all the evidence of the fixedness of species was evidence against Darwinism. The absence of intermediate forms in the fossil record was a criticism Darwin was unable to answer, and the inability of humans to breed hybrids led even Thomas Huxley to declare Darwin's doctrine only an hypothesis, not worthy to be called a theory.[19]

In the end, however, it was not these scientific objections that led Hodge against Darwinism. What made it impossible for him to accept the theory was its naturalism. "The grand and fatal objection to Darwinism," he wrote, "is the exclusion of design." Even though Darwin believed in a Creator, or at least did when he published *The Origin of Species*, that creator merely called matter and a living germ into existence and then let life be controlled by chance and necessity. There was no design in nature, no intelligence behind the selection of characteristics. Hodge found this characterisation of nature simply flying in the face of reason. In numerous examples in the style of Paley, Hodge challenged the reader with the sheer unlikeliness that the beautifully balanced living world could happen without any guidance. "[I]n thus denying design in nature, these writers array against themselves the intuitive perceptions and irresistible convictions of all mankind—a barrier which no man has ever been able to surmount."[20] Yet Darwin and his admirers preferred the operation of chance to the operation of God, and indeed "the most extreme of Mr Darwin's admirers adopt and laud his theory for the special reason that it banished God from the world".[21]

Darwin's theory denied design in nature, and in Hodge's opinion to deny design in nature was to deny God. Therefore, Darwinian evolution was atheistic. Hodge could not reconcile the two; but he did acknowledge that there were Christians who accepted evolution. What did he say of them? Any evolutionist who was also a Christian was, by definition, not a Darwinian. The concept of evolution was not the problem; a denial of God, was.

B. B. Warfield: a Darwinian of the purest water

Benjamin B. Warfield, who took the chair of theology at Princeton (previously Hodge's) in 1887, shared with Hodge the conviction that science and religion could not be at odds. He and Hodge were, in fact, from precisely the same theological tradition, and can be regarded as close allies in defense of Biblical truth. It was on this very subject that Warfield wrote for *The Fundamentals*. Yet where Hodge concluded "Darwinism is atheism", Warfield described himself at one point in his career as "a Darwinian of the purest water".[22] How could these two, with such similar views about science, theology and the Bible, disagree so diametrically? One factor might have been the intervening years in which evolutionary theory had became stronger in the scientific community, and in which the theory had been modified to cope with some of its defects, which to some extent answered Hodge's criticisms. Warfield still perceived several problems with the theory; he was not blindly following where scientific leaders led. Yet for all the theory's defects, he considered it a plausible account of a possible mechanism of biological development, and held that its strict naturalism (which repelled Hodge) was not necessary, and perhaps even detrimental, to the theory's explanatory power.

✢

One of the ongoing points of tension between theology and the historical sciences has been the understanding of the early chapters of the book of Genesis. Warfield was quite aware of the issue. In the paper 'On the Antiquity and the Unity of the Human Race', 1911, Warfield presented a discussion of the relationship between scientific evidence concerning the origins of the human race and how it related to Biblical evidence. The fundamental Biblical assertion was, in Warfield's words, that man owes his being to God. Yet, he commented philosophically, subsidiary questions come and go, and lately the most important of these subsidiary questions had concerned the method of the divine procedure in creating man.

Warfield's opinion of evolutionary theory was immediately obvious.

> Discussion of this question became acute on the publication of Charles Darwin's treatise on the 'Origin of Species' in 1859, and can never sink again into rest until it is thoroughly understood in all quarters that 'evolution' cannot act as a substitute for creation, but at best can supply only a theory of the method of the divine providence.[23]

Immediately we see that Warfield was happy to regard evolution as a possible mechanism used by God. Many 'theistic evolutionists' take the same position today, but the criticism usually lodged against them is how to reconcile the long periods of time in evolutionary theory with the chronology of the early chapters of the Bible. This question of time—the *antiquity* of the human race—was Warfield's concern here.

The question of the antiquity of man, Warfield stated, has no theological significance. It is to theology a matter of entire indifference how long man has existed on earth. It is only because of the contrast which has been drawn between the short period which seems to be allotted to human history in the Biblical narrative, and the tremendously long period assigned to human life by certain schools of science, that theology has become interested in the topic. Yet, claimed Warfield, the Bible does not assign a brief span to human history; this is done only by a particular mode of interpreting the biblical data—a mode he disputed. Neither does science demand an inordinate period of life; this is only one school of thought. That was why, Warfield commented, the question had for the most part, at his time, disappeared from theological discussion.

Warfield acknowledged that a *prima facie* view of the Biblical record makes the human race look recent. This, moreover, had been the usual supposition of simple Bible readers, and had become so fixed it was even printed in the Bible.[24] However, Warfield insisted, Ussher's dating is not reliable. His data rest largely on genealogies, from which it is precarious to draw chronology. For all we know, the periods of time encompassed before Abraham might have been of immense length. Genealogies in the Old Testament did not require a complete record of all the generations, but only an adequate indication of the particular line through which the descent in question comes. This is demonstrated in the genealogies of Jesus.

When we look at the early genealogies of Genesis, Warfield wrote, it is clear their purpose was not mere chronology. If that were the purpose, why is so much unnecessary information supplied? We only gain the impression of chronology from their sequence. It had been argued that the fact that the ages of individuals are included indicates that these lists constitute a chronology (for instance, when we are told how old people were when their children were born; see, for example, Genesis chapter 5). This, however, Warfield regarded as a specious argument. If it read "Adam was eight cubits in height and begat Seth; and Seth was seven cubits in height and begat Enosh" we would regard the remarks as purely parenthetical. The fact that we are told people's ages might mean only that we are to be impressed by their longevity. In other words, the Scriptural data leave us wholly without guidance in estimating the time which elapsed between the creation of the world and the deluge, and between the deluge and Abraham.

Therefore, the question of the antiquity of man was purely a scientific one, as far as Warfield was concerned. As an interested observer, however, the theologian could make two comments. The first was that science has no solid data for a definite estimate of the time during which the human race existed; the second was that the time estimates were coming down. The very long estimates of time were due to Darwin's particular type of gradualism, which asserted minute changes over immense periods of time that would gradually build up to changes in species. By Warfield's time, he observed, it was thought that these minute changes were not enough, and the theory of evolution was changing, and so the pressures on the time estimates were being relieved.[25]

These ideas were explored further in a careful review Warfield published in 1908 of a recent book called *Darwinism Today*, by Vernon Kellog.[26] Kellog was an evolutionist, and an open opposer of Christian thinking, who wrote to defend evolutionary theory against its critics. While openly acknowledging the weaknesses and disagreements within evolutionary biology, his conclusion was that evolution was solidly established and he looked forward to a time when further research would solve all its problems of detail. The book gave an overview of evolutionary theories, explaining the problems in the theories and the methods proposed by different scientists to overcome them. In reviewing Kellog's book, Warfield was provided with the forum to explain his opinion of evolutionary theory, and more importantly to explain his attitude towards the scientific method of thinking of which Kellog was both representative and defender. For in the end, Warfield's opinion of the theory was little different from Kellog's own. The difference arose in the conclusions each drew, and the way in which (in Warfield's opinion) scientific thinking was biased by a rigid adherence to a naturalistic world-view.

By 1907, the year of publication of Kellog's book, evolutionists had in Kellog's opinion moved beyond the theory explained by Darwin. A significant number of biologists had revolted against the view that natural selection had the capacity for species-forming. Kellog himself held that natural selection had a very important function in species selection but denied its omnipotence. Warfield agreed with this analysis. The theory of evolution by natural selection in its most basic form, as far as he could tell, looked simple and convincing. As soon as it was transformed into the realm of fact, however, difficulties arose. Some of the objections that have been raised in Kellog's book were, in Warfield's view, *not* valid, and here we actually find Warfield defending Darwinism against unnecessary attacks. For instance, it had been claimed that the theory was inconsistent or incomplete as a logical construction. It was objected that it provided only for the survival of the fittest, not for the production of the fittest, leaving unexplained the whole matter of the cause of variation. Yet Warfield rejected this as missing the point.

> The Darwinian theory does not need to concern itself with the origin of the fittest, the cause of variation, the causes of the specific variations which occur or their opportuneness or consecution. It is logically complete in the simple postulates of variation, struggle for existence, the survival of the fittest.[27]

Logically speaking, the theory was quite plausible.

No, wrote Warfield, the problem with the theory of natural selection only arises when it is assumed that this process has actually taken place. What reason is there to believe that the struggle for existence in nature is severe enough to eliminate in each generation all but the fittest? What reason is there to suppose that the differences are great enough to be telling? What reason to suppose that, even if natural selection occurs, this process will result in any great modification rather than successive generations fluctuating around a centre? What reason is there to suppose that divergence could advance very far in the time at disposal—especially when you consider how very far it has to go? These were the problems, and Kellog had for the most part acknowledged them. Though technically plausible, "the formal completeness of the logical theory of Darwinism is fairly matched, therefore, by its almost ludicrous actual incompetence of the work asked of it."[28]

Such problems had been recognised in the scientific community of the time, to the extent that Kellog described strict Darwinism—differentiation by natural selection on small differences over a long time—as "seriously discredited in the biological world".[29] Why, then, was the theory still so popular? Because, answered Warfield, there was nothing to take its place.

> No one of these [alternative theories] will serve any better than Darwinism itself serves—possibly not even so well as Darwinism serves—as a complete 'causo-mechanical' explanation of the differentiation of organic forms...The problem still presses on us; a great variety of suggestions are being made to solve it; it remains as yet unsolved.[30]

Yet Kellog, who recognised the need for modification of the theory, dismissed out of hand any theory with any hint of a guiding principle (which Kellog named 'mysticism'). Here, Warfield made his major complaint against Kellog and the scientific community he represented. Despite the problems with evolutionary theory, here was a prominent scientist unwilling to consider a suggestion which might solve some of the problems. Even though a 'guiding principle' could take a number of forms, none were acceptable to Kellog. This Warfield could not approve, for it constituted in his opinion a rather polemic attitude towards teleology.

This gives the disagreeable appearance to the trend

of biological speculation—we do not say of biological investigation—that it is less interested in science for science's sake, that is, in the increase of knowledge, than it is in the validation of a naturalistic world-view; that it is dominated, in a word, by philosophical conceptions, not derived from science but imposed on science from without.[31]

Warfield was not against evolution; his point was that to deny all teleology, to insist on pure accidentalism, was not only unscientific but detrimental in practice to the theory. The initial strict form of Darwinism had been thoroughly anti-teleological, he agreed, but given the explanatory problems this strictness had created, surely it was time to move beyond that. It was not as if teleology were unscientific, or failed to deal with problems of causation.

> Some lack of general philosophical acumen must be suspected when it is not fully understood that teleology is in no way inconsistent with—is rather necessarily involved in—a complete system of natural causation. Every teleological system implies a complete 'causo-mechanical' explanation as its instrument.[32]

In the meantime, it seemed that scientific thought was under the control of anti-teleological prejudice; and it did not take much acumen to suggest that this was in fact an anti-theistic prejudice.

Warfield affirmed the logical plausibility of evolution, while maintaining firmly that the version of the theory currently accepted needed to undergo change. Warfield's understanding of these weaknesses in the theory made him not at all embarrassed to posit a guiding principle to evolution, not just to support his biblical understanding, but in response to some of the strictly scientific problems which the theory seemed unable to overcome on a naturalistic basis. He believed evolution could have happened, as a process guided by God. At this point, Hodge would presumably have insisted that Warfield was therefore not a Darwinian. In this sense he was not, for he rejected ateleological evolution. Yet it is interesting that in this case at least, he rejected it for its scientific problems—the very problems recognised by the scientific community itself—not because of his theological belief. Indeed, it could be said that his theological position left him open to a greater range of scientific theories, for he did not have the innate prejudice against teleology that in his opinion was hampering the biological community of the time.

James Orr: Sin

Finally we turn to the Scot, James Orr, who with Warfield was one of the original fundamentalists. In fact, two of his four essays for *The Fundamentals* dealt with evolutionary issues—one on the relationship between science and religion, and evolution in particular, and another on the interpretation of the early chapters of Genesis.[33] Both were favourable towards evolution; but Orr is an interesting writer for another reason. Not only did he deal with the problem of evolutionary theory in relation to the Bible, or evolutionary theory and its internal scientific problems, he also dealt with the theological problem of sin. This is an issue not so often raised in the science and religion debate. It goes beyond interpretation of the early chapters of Genesis, and even beyond the general problem of design. If evolution is true, was there ever a morally uncorrupted state and an historical fall? When and how can a biblical mankind in the image of God, morally responsible and different from animals, fit into the story of evolutionary development?

In 1910 Orr published *Sin as a Problem of Today*, in which he presented the biblical problem of sin and, amongst other external considerations, discussed the relationship of this doctrine with evolutionary theory. The doctrine of sin, he realised, was under threat. This was a serious problem; for without the doctrine of sin, the Christian doctrine of redemption through Christ is meaningless. At this point, the theologian must comment on where science is taking humanity.

> The theologian may be to blame when he rashly or dogmatically intrudes into the domain of science; on the other hand, it is not his place to be silent when the scientists make bold inroads into *his* domain, and, in the name of science, would sweep away spiritual facts which stand on their own grounds of evidence as securely as any facts of external nature. Truths in nature and truths in the spiritual world, cannot, of course, be in real collision. But this requires to be made clear against unwarrantable assertion on either side.[34]

Orr did not consider himself an expert in science, claiming "no more than the right of every intelligent mind to consider theories of science as expounded by their best representatives in the light of their own evidence."[35] He did not wish to dispute evolution, merely to plead for its being kept within its scientific limits. His firm conviction was that very little that is truly scientific conflicts with Christian beliefs about man's nature, origin and sin.

First he had to present an evaluation of the current state of evolutionary theory, and here Orr differed little from Warfield in both his appreciation and his criticisms of the theory. Evolution in some form is an old idea, Orr wrote. Hegel was an evolutionist as truly as Darwin, but the forms their evolution took were very different. Darwin gave evolution scientific precision and connected it with a theory of the "how"; namely, natural selection. Orr stated it plainly: "The *fact* of evolution is now generally accepted: the *how*, it will be found, is still much in debate."[36] Like Warfield, Orr demanded some room for doubt: "Is 'natural selection', or any purely 'causal-mechanical' theory, an adequate account of evolution?"[37]

Darwinism, wrote Orr in a now familiar strain, is firstly characterised by its naturalism. Natural selection, acting on unguided variations, under the conditions of the struggle for existence, brings about the adaptation which people formerly supposed to imply the presence of mind. Theologians (and perhaps he was here thinking of Hodge) did not misrepresent Darwin in speaking of his theory as essentially opposed to theism. Many evolutionists modify this naturalism and so desert Darwin. However, the mainstream of evolutionary thought is unfavourable to a religious interpretation of nature. Nature can work out all her results without the aid of intelligence or purpose. Teleology is eliminated, and so God becomes a superfluous hypothesis. If the universe can be explained without intelligence—and Darwinism contends that the universe can be so explained—then why postulate intelligence? Man very slowly evolved, under forces of nature, by natural selection, until by degrees he attained civilisation.

It is clear, Orr went on, that this strikes deeply at the doctrine of sin. It is not just that the theory eliminates God; but the theory itself supposes man did not 'appear' at one time, but that there was an imperceptible gradation from apes to man. The concept of an historical fall must go, under this schema; man, instead of having fallen, has 'risen'. What is more, the very idea of sin is essentially altered. Sin is no longer "the voluntary defection of a creature who had the power to remain sinless."[38] On the contrary, sin becomes "a natural necessity of man's ascent".[39] The idea of guilt vanishes, as does the idea of a lost world needing redemption. What has been called hereditary sin is merely the "yet uneliminated brute inheritance."[40]

It is no solution, Orr urged, to try to rewrite the Old Testament and excise the doctrine of sin. The doctrine is there, clearly taught. The question is, can the early chapters of Genesis be accounted for in harmony with a Darwinian view of man? Many theologians say yes, arguing that at some point the developing man gained a moral sense, and then the moral crisis—the Fall—occurred. Orr did not consider this tenable. Existence as a miserable animal ruled by instinct can hardly be conceived of as a state of purity from which we fell. It was not within Orr's conception of the image of God to allow that a 'missing-link' ape-like being "whose nature is in violent turbulence, whose life is brutish, who has not even the glimmer of a right knowledge of God"[41] could be the original man described by Scripture. Naturalism does not even allow the free will to choose between good and evil.[42] The developing being, a brute acting on impulse, cannot be found guilty since he is merely acting according to unreasoning nature.

Evolutionary theory, then, was opposed to the Biblical idea of sin as voluntary departure from God's rule. "We seem thus to be brought to an *impasse*",[43] Orr wrote with delicate emphasis. Do we reject the Biblical doctrine of sin, confirmed by the experience of ages, or the doctrine of evolution, which science has almost universally accepted as the truth? "Neither alternative", Orr insists, "can be entertained." Sin is real, and although evolution has not been strictly proved, its evidence is very strong. "The proof for some form of organic evolution, within limits, is peculiarly cogent."[44] The solution, Orr sees, lies in the way in which evolution is understood.

Evolutionary theory had changed from Darwin's time to the time Orr was writing, which we have already seen to some extent in the discussion of

Warfield. Strict Darwinism was no longer followed, according to Orr, who wrote of the "remarkable, sometimes revolutionary, changes which have taken place on this subject".[45] The controversy was over the capacity for natural selection *alone* to account for organic life. The sufficiency of natural selection to account for the phenomena of nature was assumed, not proved; and what is more, assumed on the grounds that only natural causation can be admitted. "Religion," Orr wryly remarked, "plainly is not the only thing which makes a demand on faith."[46]

It was not disputed, and neither did Orr dispute, that "variability, struggle for existence, natural selection, and heredity, have much to do with the process of evolution".[47] What was questioned in scientific circles was the sufficiency of these causes. Newer evolutionary thought apparently looked to internal causes, which pointed to there being direction in evolution. That is, prominent evolutionists were now writing of abrupt and discontinuous mutations, that would make evolution proceed by leaps.[48] In this case, the effect of natural selection—environmental pressures acting on minute changes—would be less prominent, and the causality of evolution would come from within. A further problem noted by contemporary evolutionists was doubt about the strength of the struggle for existence; and the insufficiency of natural selection to carry out the enormous tasks assigned to it, when natural selection was not a creative but an eliminative agency.

Such objections could be answered, Orr realised,

more or less plausibly. Yet the cumulative effect of the problems was great, enough to throw severe doubt on the naturalistic and ateleological form of the theory.

> Evolutionist writers claim large rights of scepticism for themselves. They must permit some right of scepticism to others when asking them to believe that a blind force of the kind supposed is really the main explanation of the beauty and adaptation with which the world is filled.[49]

There was pressure, then, to move back to teleology. Science, as well as theology, was giving testimony to the necessity for the concept of purpose in nature.

The outcome of this review of the current state of evolutionary theory was to leave Orr more optimistic about the implications of evolution. Sin is incompatible with the strict naturalism of Darwinism; but if evolution is guided—and not necessarily slow, but proceeding with sudden mutations which introduce new factors—then the problem is changed. It may not be possible to *prove* that original man was sinless, but there is now room for such an origin. It is possible that there might have been a sudden jump to man, a new kind of being. The question becomes one, not of theory, but of evidence.

It is no objection, wrote Orr, to insist that evolution, working through natural processes, cannot be compatible with creation by God. An explanation of mechanism does not *per se* exclude God, for God could have easily worked through a mechanism: "no one supposes that man is less a creature of God because he owes his existence, mediately, to a long line of ancestors".[50] From a theistic viewpoint it did not matter whether the creative power was latent in nature, only waiting the appropriate time for its manifestation, or whether fresh drafts of creative power were infused directly and periodically. This was no antithesis to evolution. What is more, there was evidence that man *did* arise in a leap; "The great gulf between man and lower forms stands still unbridged."[51]

On a metaphysical note, Orr observed that a supernaturally guided evolution was necessary to account for the existence of moral activity. Naturalistic evolutionary theory assumes that the same causes which are held adequate to explain the bodily development of man also explain the higher mental powers—but is this adequate? Most writers acknowledged a difference between the rationality of man and animals, particularly in the capacity for ethics:

> Selfhood, personality, moral freedom, the supreme value of moral ends, require a spiritual basis, and mean, not simply development, but the setting up of a new order of kingdom of being in the universe.[52]

Naturalistic evolution cannot explain this. "The conclusion is that, with every wish to give evolution its fullest rights, it cannot be pronounced adequate to explain the moral and spiritual dignity of man."[53] In other words, Orr was willing to accept evolution as true, but insufficient. It could not adequately explain humanity.

Orr's conclusion, far from being a defensive rearrangement of his Christian beliefs to fit in with evolution, was a generous concession to evolution despite its inadequacies. "In fine [in conclusion], it is not to be denied that evolutionary theory, great as may be its services, leaves us with the main problems as regards origins as yet unsolved...The time has clearly not yet come for dogmatically ruling out the Christian presuppositions of a doctrine of sin."[54]

✠

We have seen here examples of Christian reasoning about evolution. None of their arguments prove whether or not evolution is true, and individuals may be more or less convinced by any particular argument. Since then, further discoveries have been added to the scientific repertoire, such as a better understanding of genetics and the possibility of mutation.[55] At the same time, some of the criticisms these men made of evolution are still valid; for instance, the question of whether it proceeded by gradual change or sudden jumps remains, as many aspects of the fossil record appear better explained by the sudden appearance of new forms.[56]

Yet the particular arguments here advanced for or against evolution are not the point. The point is that these intelligent critiques of evolutionary theory, which take its scientific value seriously, are astonishing given modern caricatures of fundamentalism. Historically it is not true that fundamentalist Christianity, as that which is most committed to integrity and honest acceptance of the Bible, is anti-science, or even necessarily anti-evolution. It is not true that the original fundamentalists were anti-intellectual, blinkered dogmatists. Neither is it true that evolution is proved beyond doubt and beyond question, or is in a fixed and final form. The evolutionary debate could do with a strong infusion of open-mindedness, honest acknowledgment of uncertainty, and preparedness to change ill-conceived prejudices. Hodge, Warfield and Orr were able to examine the question openly and present their point of view in such a spirit.

ENDNOTES

1   Vernon L. Kellog, *Darwinism Today: A Discussion of Present-Day Scientific Criticism of the Darwinian Selection Theories, Together with a Brief Account of the principal other Proposed Auxiliary and Alternative Theories of Species-Forming,* George Bell and Sons, London, Henry Holt and Company, New York, 1907, p. 5.

2   Quoted in Mark A. Noll and David Livingstone (eds), *Charles Hodge: What is Darwinism? And Other Writings on Science and Religion,* Baker Books, Grand Rapids, 1994, p. 42. This is how Warfield described himself as an undergraduate.

3   This series was published between 1910 and 1915, and sent free of charge to a wide range of Christian leaders, in order to defend what were considered the 'fundamentals' of Christian faith.

4   There is a considerable literature about 'Fundamentalism' as a phenomena. It is analysed sociologically, politically and philosophically, and frequently written about almost entirely independently of its historical religious background. This essay is not a comment on this modern literature, which is far removed from the practice of using 'fundamentalist' as merely a label for anti-intellectualism.

5   There is still much work to be done in this field. More primary sources can be found in Mark A. Noll (ed.), *The Princeton Theology 1812-1921: Scripture, Science, and Theological Method from Archibald Alexander to Benjamin Breckinridge Warfield,* Baker Book

House, Grand Rapids, 1983. A closer analysis of Hodge's work can be found in Jonathon Wells, *Charles Hodge's Critique of Darwinism. An Historical-Critical Analysis of Concepts Basic to the 19th Century Debate,* The Edwin Mellen Press, Lewiston, 1988. For discussion of science and religion in America see Jon H. Roberts, *Darwinism and the Divine in America: Protestant Intellectuals and Organic Evolution, 1859-1900,* University of Wisconsin Press, Madison, 1988 and David N. Livingstone, *Darwin's Forgotten Defenders,* William B. Eerdmans and Scottish Academic Press, 1987. The general literature on Darwin and reactions to his ideas is immense, and the endnotes here mention only a few easily accessible and well known works. Other references which provide a starting point to research are: Alvar Ellegard, *Darwin and the General Reader: The Reception of Darwin's Theory of Evolution in the British Periodical Press, 1859-1872,* The University of Chicago Press, Chicago and London, 1958-1990 and David Hull, *Darwin and His Critics: The Reception of Darwin's Theory of Evolution by the Scientific Community,* Harvard University Press, Cambridge, Mass., 1973. One of the best biographies of Darwin is Adrian Desmond and James Moore, *Darwin,* Michael Joseph, London, 1991.

6   At this time the conservative tradition which made Princeton so influential moved with J. Gresham Machen to Westminster Theologial Seminary, which he helped found.

7   A letter to the editors of the *New York Observer,* January 1863; reproduced in Noll and Livingstone *op. cit.,* pp. 53-56.

8   *Ibid.,* p. 55.

9   In the United States in the decades after Darwin a group of 'Neo-Lamarckian' evolutionists were very influential (following the ideas of Lamarck, the famous French naturalist who postulated evolution through the inheritance of acquired characteristics). They were lead by Alpheus Hyatt (1838-1902), Alpheus S. Packard Jr (1839-1905) and Edward Drinker Cope (1840-1897), and included several other naturalists, botanists and geologists, and zoologists. To them, natural selection was merely one of a series of factors which make up a true evolution theory. See James R. Moore, *The Post-Darwinian Controversies: A Study of the Protestant Struggle to Come to Terms with Darwin in Great Britain and America, 1870-1900,* Cambridge University Press, Cambridge, 1979, chapter 6.

10   Noll and Livingstone, *op. cit.,* p. 66.

11   Hodge cites Darwin saying that Dr W. C. Wells in 1813 "distinctly recognises the principle of natural selection", and that Patrick Matthew in 1831 "gives precisely the same view of the origin of species as that propounded by Mr Wallace and myself". See *ibid.,* p. 91 and the editorial note. For an account of other earlier evolutionary theories, see D. R. Oldroyd, *Darwinian Impacts: An Introduction to the Darwinian Revolution,* New South Wales University Press, Kensington, 1980.

12   Noll and Livingstone, *op. cit.,* p. 92.

13   *Ibid.,* p. 131.

14   *Ibid.*

15   *Ibid.,* p. 133.

16   *Ibid.,* p. 135.

17   *Ibid.,* p. 140. Such an expression of utter astonishment was common in the early days of Darwinian theory. These days, such expressions are dismissed as the "argument from incredulity" by evolutionist writers such as Richard Dawkins. At this point Dawkins is precisely right; the fact that we cannot comprehend something is no argument for its untruth. Many bizarre things are true. Nevertheless, it is interesting to speculate whether the decrease in incredulity about Darwinism is due to increased confidence in the theory, or just familiarity with its astounding claims. An argument from credulity is no more valid than one from incredulity.

18   *Vestiges of the Natural History of Creation* was published anonymously by Robert Chambers in 1844. It must be taken into account that *Vestiges* was an amateur work with nothing like the solid scientific value of Darwin's book; nevertheless Hodge's point is a valid one and demonstrates his awareness of the way in which the acceptance of a scientific theory can be ideologically driven.

19   The fossil record does not reveal gradual transformations of structure; it shows species remaining much the same over time, to be replaced by new forms. Darwin's answer, and one still popular, is that the fossil record preserved only a tiny fraction of living animals, with the added hope that eventually transformational forms will be found.

Thomas Huxley, who earned the nickname "Darwin's bulldog" for his passionate defence of Darwinism, was nevertheless not convinced of the power of natural selection alone to create species, for there were no examples of mutually infertile new breeds created by artificial selection (dog breeders can produce big dogs or sleek dogs, but they are still dogs.) On the other hand, Darwin and other working naturalists considered the proof of natural selection to be in its predictive and explanatory power so did not find the question of breeding hybrids a problem. See Moore, *op. cit.,* pp. 176-77.

20 Noll and Livingstone, *op.cit.,* p. 153.

21 *Ibid.,* p. 155.

22 Quoted in *ibid.,* p. 42.

23 B. B. Warfield, 'On the Antiquity and Unity of the Human Race', *Studies in Theology,* Oxford University Press, 1932; Baker Book House, Grand Rapids, 1981, p. 235. This paper was originally published in *The Princeton Theological Review,* 1911.

24 Bishop James Ussher (1581-1656) had calculated a scriptural chronology and claimed that the creation had to be in 4004 BC. This date was later printed in the marginal notes of the Authorized Version of the Bible.

25 William Thomson (1824-1907) published physical arguments which placed radical constraints on the geologists' estimates of time. He argued that given known cooling rates, the earth was too warm to be millions of years old. Thomson thought the limited time was sufficient to disprove evolution by natural selection. Since then, radioactive material has been discovered which explains why the temperature of the earth is still so high; Thomson obviously could not have known about this extra source of energy.

26 Kellog, *op. cit.* Warfield's review can be found in *Critical Reviews,* Oxford University Press, 1932; Baker Book House, Grand Rapids, 1981. This paper was originally published in *The Princeton Theological Review,* 1908.

27 Warfield *ibid.,* p. 181. The cause of variation was one of the most cited problems with Darwin's theory. Whence does the variation come for natural selection to work on? For Darwin's theory to work, variations have to continue to appear without limit. Most of Darwin's colleagues believed that the extent of

variation in every organism tends to be strictly limited. H. C. Jenkin, a mathematician, maintained on the basis of experimental evidence that each animal or plant is contained within a 'sphere of variation'. To answer his critics, Darwin allowed a degree of Larmarkianism. See Moore, *op. cit.*, chapter 5.

28 Warfield, *ibid.*, p. 183.

29 *Ibid.*, p. 184, quoting Kellog *op. cit.*, p. 5. Kellog listed numerous scientific objections to Darwinism. The main ones were: problems of variation (its origin; whether variations are large enough to give any survival advantage; and the problem of useless characteristics); the problem of inheritance (that favourable variations would be lost through interbreeding; and the necessity for several structures to develop simultaneously); that geologic time was too short; and the linear nature of fluctuation (variations seem to accumulate along certain lines; and although selection explains adaptive change it does not necessarily explain diversity into species). Darwin had had answers to most of these problems, but large parts of the biological community were not convinced. However, there was no alternative of sufficient explanatory power to take the place of natural selection. Today, some of these problems have been solved by better understanding of genetics and mutation which causes variation.

30 Warfield, *ibid,* p. 184.. The 'alternative theories' canvassed by Kellog were: Lamarckian inheritance of acquired characteristics; orthogenesis, which posited some guiding principle to evolution (whether internal or environmental); and heterogenesis, which postulated large evolutionary jumps through mutations. These theories could overlap, and some evolutionists took bits of each or combinations of these with natural selection.

31 *Ibid.*, p. 189.

32 *Ibid.*

33 *The Fundamentals* also contained an essay 'The passing of evolution', by George Frederick Wright, which criticised the weak points of Darwinian evolution while remaining open to evolution itself, and rejected the atheism with which Darwinian evolution was associated.

34 James Orr, *Sin as a Problem of Today,* Hodder and Stoughton, London, 1910, p. 130.

35   Ibid., pp. 130-31.

36   Ibid., p. 133.

37   Ibid.

38   Ibid., p. 139.

39   Ibid.

40   Ibid.

41   Ibid., p. 144

42   An interesting idea which is a key issue in the debate between determinism and free will.

43   Orr, op, cit., p. 148.

44   Ibid., p. 149.

45   Ibid.

46   Ibid., p. 152.

47   Ibid.

48   Huxley had always preferred the idea of evolution by leaps. He thought Darwin unnecessarily hampered himself by insisting on minute variations accumulating over a vast time; the main problem being, as seen before, the need for a continual supply of new variations.

49   Ibid., p. 159.

50   Ibid., p. 168.

51   Ibid., p. 175.

52   Ibid., p. 182.

53   Ibid., p. 183.

54   Ibid., p. 194.

55   See David J. Depew and Bruce H. Weber, Darwinism Evolving: Systems Dynamics and the Genealogy of Natural Selection, MIT Press, Cambridge, Mass., 1995.

56   For a modern defence of evolutionary theory, see D. R. Selkirk and F. J. Burrows (eds), Confronting Creationism: Defending Darwin, The New South Wales University Press, Kensington, 1987; Stephen Jay Gould has written numerous general essays, a good starting point being his Ever Since Darwin: Reflections in Natural History, Penguin Books, Harmondsworth, 1977. Modern critiques of the theory are found in Michael Denton, Evolution: A Theory in Crisis, Adler and Adler, Bethesda, 1985; and Phillip E. Johnson, Darwin on Trial, Intervarsity Press, Downers Grove, 1993.

6.
History gone wrong: the Scopes trial

Kirsten Birkett

IN 1925, JOHN Scopes was arrested for teaching evolution in his high-school biology class in the small town of Dayton, Tennessee. He was tried and found guilty, and fined $100. The trial was over within a few days. The law was eventually repealed. It doesn't seem all that funny.

Yet this trial is one of the major reasons why creationism, and belief in the Bible in general, became a laughing-stock in America and places where American culture rules. It provided a huge intellectual blow to the credibility of sincere Christian belief and made 'fundamentalist' virtually synonymous with 'stupid'. Because of this event, evolution gained massive public acceptance not just as a true theory, but as an alternative to biblical creation and one which made belief in the Bible outdated and childish.

Summer for the Gods,[*] Edward J. Larson's 1998 Pulitzer Prize-winning book about the Scopes trial, is for the

---

[*] This article was originally published as an essay review of Edward J. Larson, *Summer for the Gods: The Scopes Trial and America's Continuing Debate over Science and Religion*, BasicBooks, New York, 1997.

most part documentation of precisely what happened before, during, and after the trial. It is not written with any overt partisan leanings, and indeed is rather dry in its lengthy descriptions of who did what on which day and with what result. It is a book that tells a surprising story; for the trial in reality bears little resemblance to the trial I had read about, even in Christian books. It is a startling testament to how a mythology can take hold of public awareness to the point where even those hurt by the mythology do not question its truth. Through the dramatisations of the Scopes trial and the way in which it was remembered in American written history, the actual trial has been almost totally obscured, and reading what really happened is a profoundly shocking and delightful experience.

The myth I had believed was that defence lawyer Clarence Darrow, evolutionist, had confronted fundamentalist prosecutor William Jennings Bryan over the Bible, and shown him up as a fool; this was the essence of the trial. I had been embarrassed on behalf of the Christians (why didn't they choose an intelligent man to defend them?) and reluctantly admiring of the cool rational Darrow (at least he had reason on his side) and sympathetic for John Scopes, the poor teacher prosecuted for teaching what he thought was true.

It was, after all, what I had been taught, in numerous books, newspaper columns and lectures. Received history testified that biblical belief, and the blind prejudice of its supporters, was in the Scopes trial finally forced out into the scientific light of day and shown up for the inanity it is. When it came to the crunch, the Bible just could not stand up against the facts of science. Although narrow-minded churchgoers had tried to use the weight of the law to stop the progress of science—as they had with Galileo—this time, science finally won. You just can't stop progress.

The metaphor of the church as a tyrannical overlord standing against the freedom of scientific inquiry is an old one. It drags from the Middle Ages to Galileo; it follows Descartes' fear of publishing his philosophy in Catholic France; it props up Darwin as he faced a church backlash against his theory; it carries Soapy Sam Wilberforce into battle—and ignominious defeat—against Thomas Huxley; and it appears again in the Scopes trial. It's one particular aspect of the general belief that science is and must be opposed by Christianity. Much publicised events like key legal trials suit the metaphor admirably, for there the battle is easily portrayed as institutional power against freedom of thought and speech, whatever the more subtle details of the case.

It is interesting that the same metaphor was not generally applied in coverage of a more recent example of this clash. The difference this time was that the side attempting to bring legal power to stop the teaching of a certain intellectual point of view was the side of science. Ian Plimer, an ardent evolutionist, took Allen Roberts of the Ark Search Inc (an extreme example of Creation Science) to court in 1997 for "misleading and deceptive conduct". Other modern evolutionists have been equally keen. Daniel Dennett has written against the teaching of creation science as the "deliberate mis-informing of children about the natural world", which should be stopped because "misinforming a child is a terrible offense".[1] It's an ironic request, since it echoes the exact rhetoric used by those who framed the original Tennessee statute against teaching evolution on which John Scopes was prosecuted. Do not teach as true, the parents of Tennessee demanded, these unproven ideas which damage our children.

However, few people today would ever have heard what the parents of Tennessee said. The real arguments of the people involved in the Scopes Trial have all but disappeared. Somehow, the safety-grids for preserving truth in our society have slipped, and what people now know or think about the Scopes Trial is not what really happened. Instead of truth, an anti-religion rhetoric has survived, and apparently has survived for no better reason than that it *is* anti-religion. Those who should have known better—academics who should have researched original documents before teaching their students, education boards who should have reviewed the material they recommended—failed to live up to their positions. The guardians of truth failed to realise that what they were teaching was inaccurate, because they were comfortable with it.

✦

If our usual understanding of the Scopes trial is illusion, then what was the reality? William Jennings Bryan, advocate of anti-evolution laws and counsel for the prosecution during the trial, was essentially a career politician. He was a one time Secretary of State who negotiated fiercely for a series of international treaties before the first world war, designed to avert war by requiring the arbitration of disputes among nations. He resigned from his office at the start of the first world war, but continued to campaign for constitutional amendments, and was successful in four particular amendments: the direct election of senators, a progressive federal income tax, Prohibition, and female suffrage. He was no fool, and no stranger to fierce public political argument. His opposition to Darwinism was largely on moral grounds; although he accepted the possibility of a long process of creation as being consistent with the Bible, he objected to the implications of Darwinistic philosophy.

> I object to the Darwinian theory because I fear we shall lose the consciousness of God's presence in our daily life, if we must accept the theory that through all the ages no spiritual force has touched the life of man and shaped the destiny of nations...But there is another objection. The Darwinian theory represents man as reaching his present perfection by the operation of the law of hate—the merciless law by which the strong crowd out and kill off the weak (quoted p. 39).

When two scholarly works were published after the first world war which attributed German militarism to misguided Darwinian thinking, Bryan became even more opposed to Darwinism. It was argued that the idea of natural selection based on violent competitive struggle strongly influenced German intellectualism; Darwin's influence on Nietzsche was also considered significant. Bryan also saw a connection between Darwinism and the breaking down of Christian belief in the universities. Darwinism, Bryant believed, was a danger to individuals, to society and to world peace. He was not alone, and probably persuaded many more through his itinerant speaking. When the Tennessee House of Representatives was presented with the bill against teaching evolution—or rather against teaching "any theory that denies the story of the Divine Creation of man as taught in the Bible, and to teach instead that man had descended from a lower order of animal" (quoted p. 50), the bill was passed seventy-one to five.

✝

It was the American Civil Liberties Union who provided the initiative for the trial to challenge this bill. The ACLU had fought a wide range of issues, including the right to conscientious objection during the war—in fact to a large extent it had been founded and financed by Quakers to protect religiously motivated pacifists from compulsory military service. After the first world war, the ACLU turned its attention to protecting labour unions (including school teachers), and the issues of academic freedom, and freedom of speech.

When the Tennessee law was enacted, the ACLU saw it as a chance for a legal victory for freedom of speech. The leaders sent out a press release offering to challenge the law, and calling for any Tennessee teacher to volunteer as a test case. They would provide the legal defence and cover all costs, and were sure that the teacher concerned need not lose his or her job.

This was not a battle over religion. If anything, it was a battle over different forms of democracy. Bryan, who had spent his life campaigning for democracy as the fairest and most humane way to govern society, passionately believed that what the majority had voted for was what the law should uphold. In this particular case, he had further moral reasons for his conviction—he had seen that Darwinism did actually harm the moral development of young people and of society as a whole. His democracy was built upon the "virtuous citizen", and he worried that Darwinism would justify an "economic jungle" and discourage "those who labour for the improvement of man's condition".[2] He wanted to stop evolution, an unproven hypothesis, from being taught as true, especially as it was claimed to disprove Christian belief and establish materialism. When such an overwhelming majority agreed with him, he considered it merely an application of democracy to insist upon this being followed.

The ACLU members, on the other hand, did not consider democracy in this light. They considered the protection of freedom of speech as one of the most important aspects of enlightened government. Wary of censorship which could stifle dissent and the pursuit of knowledge, they considered it a democracy's duty to allow all citizens to hold their opinions—and follow their consequences—in a peaceful way. The majority vote should not be allowed to silence the minority view.

Neither side wished to debate whether evolution contradicted the Bible. However greater forces than the original combatants were moving. The motivations of the initial conflict were to be lost once other personalities with other interests entered the fray.

✠

In a small town in East Tennessee, a few young professionals gathered at the local drug store to discuss the offer from the ACLU. It seems they were struck with the possibilities of free publicity for their town. One of the group invited a close friend of his, 24-year-old John T. Scopes, to join them in one of their drug store get-togethers. He was asked if he would be willing to let his name be used for a test case. Although he was not actually a biology teacher, he had filled in for the regular teacher during an illness using the state-approved biology text, which had a section on human evolution. It was enough for the trial.

At that stage, local lawyers assumed they would be conducting the trial. However Clarence Darrow, who eventually was to be counsel for the defence at the trial, came to hear of what was going on. He was, at the time, probably the most famous trial lawyer in America. He specialised in defending criminal cases in bitterly hostile communities. One case which gained him a great deal of publicity was his defence of two wealthy and intelligent Chicago teenagers who had murdered an unpopular schoolmate. He managed to save them from the death penalty using arguments of psychological determinism.

Darrow's personal interests included public disparagement of Christianity. "In the courtroom, on the Chautauqua circuit, in public debates and lectures, and through dozens of popular books and articles, Darrow spent a lifetime ridiculing traditional Christian beliefs" (p. 71). He believed he was doing good—he considered the Christian doctrine of salvation dangerous. "It is not the bad people I fear so much as the good people. When a person is sure that he is good, he is nearly hopeless; he gets cruel—he believes in punishment" (p. 71). He was not a scientist, but he used science when it suited his purposes, just as he rejected it on other occasions when it did not.

When the Scopes trial came up, Darrow volunteered his service for the defence for free. Later he was quite open about his motivation at the time: "My object was to focus the attention of the country on the programme of Mr Bryan and the other fundamentalists in America" (p. 73). Many within the ACLU leadership were uncomfortable about Darrow's help, since he clearly had no particular interest in Scopes nor free speech in general. The ACLU had never been hostile to religion as such, and feared that Darrow's opinions might jeopardise Scope's defence. However the lawyers in Dayton welcomed such a distinguished ally, just as they welcomed Bryan as an assistant to the state for the prosecution—it just made the whole show bigger.

✠

So what was the trial about? The defendant and his local counsel were eager for the publicity. Suddenly their small town was national news, and the local businessmen expected the visitors to boost revenue considerably. Bryan considered the trial to be mainly about majority rule; about the democracy he had spent his political career defending and nurturing. It was not just a matter of whether evolution should be taught; the fact was, a large majority of the voters of Tennessee did not want it taught, and had the right to have their democratic decision abided by. The ACLU saw it as a matter of freedom of speech. Intellectual freedom must be respected in order for democracy to work at all, as they saw it. Two models of democracy were clashing.

Clarence Darrow, on the other hand, saw a chance to ridicule Christianity on a scale previously unforeseen. He gathered a battalion of professional witnesses who would testify that evolution was true. The ACLU's desire for a simple test trial disappeared under Darrow's much broader aim of having out his battle with Bryan. In the end, the ACLU was not in control of the defence at all.

Darrow nearly missed out on his wish. The expert witnesses were ruled unnecessary, the case was decided within three days. John Scopes was guilty—he had freely admitted what he taught—and there was nothing more to it. However Darrow was not to be denied all his fun. His team called Bryan as an expert on the Bible. Up until then the prosecution had strictly limited the use of expert witnesses, wanting a legal battle, not a scientific or theological one, but Bryan welcomed the opportunity to have his say and his reputation was weighty enough that he prevailed. It was the last day of the trial, and the proceedings had to be moved outside the courthouse onto the lawn to accommodate the crowds.

Darrow questioned Bryan as a hostile witness, and Bryan answered poorly. He simply did not know the answers to many of the questions on biblical detail; he was not an expert, and it became obvious under Darrow's questioning. Bryan was infuriated, and refused to step down despite his co-counsel's urging. It turned into an abusive shouting match before the judge adjourned—after two hours of interrogation. That was essentially the end of the trial; the next day the defendant was found guilty, after a few minutes deliberation by the jury.

✣

Already it is easy to see that the trial was a very complex matter. From the beginning strong personalities and private concerns were enough to distort any legal issues, and the ideological battle only made it more complicated. Perhaps the best question, then, is not to ask what was the trial about, but why did it come to be seen as a simple battle between evolution and religion, with evolution winning?

In 1931, Harper's magazine editor, Frederick Lewis Allen, published a best-selling book, *Only Yesterday: An Informal History of the Nineteen-Twenties*. It was not meant to be serious history; in the gloom of the Great

Depression, Allen was nostalgically remembering the fun of the twenties. The Scopes Trial featured as one of the largest stories of 1925. Allen pictured Darrow battling Bryan in a farcical encounter. Reducing the trial to the triumph of reason over revelation, he ignored all the wider issues, even making several factual errors in the origins of the trial, and in what Bryan said. It was the beginning of widespread misunderstanding of the trial, for Allen's book was a huge best-seller and even became widely used as a college history text. A number of later writers accepted Allen's depiction of events (p. 228).

The most serious misreporting of the trial, however, came in 1955 when *Inherit the Wind*, the play by Jerome Lawrence and Robert E. Lee, opened on Broadway. Ostensibly, their play was about the dangers of Macarthyism. Like *The Crucible*, the authors presented their ideas under the guise of a 'parallel' event in American history—this time, the Scopes Trial. Also like *The Crucible*, Christianity was taken as the parallel to mindless, irrational oppression of individuals. The fundamentalist opposition to teaching evolution was the 'metaphor' for the Macarthy opposition to freedom of writers and actors.

History was altered in several significant ways for the sake of the play. *Inherit the Wind* did not portray the trial as a comic farce, as Allen's book had, but as a dramatic, serious threat to progress and freedom. In the play—and in the later film of the same title—the ACLU and the actual reasons for the trial disappeared altogether, and a romantic interest was introduced between Scopes and the pretty daughter of a (fictitious) fire-breathing fundamentalist local pastor. There were also some major idealistic changes:

1. Scopes in the movie became the victim of a mob-enforced anti-evolution law. He was just going about his business, faithfully teaching from the textbook, when the town fathers dragged him out of the classroom and threw him into gaol, with the whole town against him. This was quite different from the real case where the defence actually instigated the trial.

2. The character representing Bryan was portrayed as a mindless, reactionary creature of the mob. He attacked evolution on narrow biblical grounds only (there was no mention of his wider social concerns) and was against all science as godless. He babbled on about the earth being created on 13 October 4004 BC at 9 am, and ended up crying to his wife in public, as well as ranting against the smallness of the fine against Scopes. (In reality, Bryan had always been opposed to there being any fine attached to the anti-evolution law. He even offered to pay the imposed fine for Scopes.)

3. Darrow was uplifted in character. He was presented as agnostic, not as a crusading materialist. In the play, Darrow angrily criticises another character who ridicules 'Bryan's' religion. This exchange, in which the other character joked that Bryan "died of a busted belly" (referring to Bryan's corpulence), is one of the few lines taken directly from real life. In real life, however, it was Darrow who said it, upon learning of Bryan's death just a few days after the trial. In stark

contrast to such callousness, the Darrow of the play and film defends Bryan's right to his religion, and chastises his colleague: "You smart-aleck! You have no more right to spit on his religion than you have a right to spit on my religion!" (pp. 242-243). He walks off with The *Origin of Species* and the Bible side-by-side in his brief-case, the model of the tolerant liberal.

The play and the movie were criticised for their inaccuracies in published reviews. Nonetheless, both remained extremely popular: the play was the then longest-running drama on Broadway, and became the accepted version of the trial. In 1994 the National Center for History in Schools published instructional standards, which recommended using excerpts from *Inherit the Wind* as part of educating students about the twenties. This process had its effect on the American consciousness, and gradually the idea that the play was actually a ridiculously distorted travesty of history drifted away. In 1996, when the play was restaged on Broadway, newspapers which had criticised the original play as "much too elementary" now praised it as "a thoughtful, powerful explication of religious and political issues". The play had not changed in the meantime—but reviewers had. They had actually come to accept that what they were seeing was a faithful representation of the issues involved in the trial. The myth had triumphed.

✢

When the Tennessee anti-evolution law was finally overturned by the Federal Supreme Court in 1967, creationists responded by demanding equal time for creationist theories. It was a logical response; the statement attributed to Darrow—"It is bigotry for public schools to teach only one theory of origins"—was now widely quoted by the creationist side. Interestingly, this statement was fictitious—part of the Scopes legend, now used by the creationists themselves. The statement is actually wrong on two counts. Not only did Darrow not say it, but creationism was never taught in schools in the twenties, because of the separation of church and state—this was even part of Bryan's attack, that if creation could not be taught then neither should evolution. The legend had well and truly by now overtaken reality. Three states attempted to have 'equal time' laws, but were all defeated—and the opponents made use of rhetoric from the Scopes legend to affect the decision.

✣

What we have in the Scopes story is a real-life example of how history was rewritten to the detriment of Christian belief, and in a surprisingly short space of time. I can remember marking a university essay about the Scopes trial. The student had described it as *Inherit the Wind*—not even realising, apparently, that his research had totally failed to report reality rather than fiction. His education had been taken over by Hollywood.

The debate between science and religion is a philosophically serious one. How can we proceed, however, when the discourse has been so seriously hijacked by false reporting? We may hope that this weighty book might have an impact—the fact that it won a Pulitzer Prize might mean that its ideas have been fairly well publicised.

Nonetheless so far I have found rather a paucity of reviews of the book; none of the main history of science journals appear to have reviewed it. Those reviews which have appeared show a sad deference to the myth. While the review in *The New York Times Book Review*[3] admits that *Inherit the Wind* "loosely fictionalized" the trial, it still ends with the recommendation "For the trial of the century, rent the movie"—no doubt tongue-in-cheek, but an annoying refusal to emphasise how misleading the movie is. A review in *The Journal of American History*[4] comments "Though Darrow's cross-examination of Bryan and the verdict in the case are already well known in American history"—ignoring Larson's demonstration that the the story is obviously *not* well known. No review I have seen takes seriously the challenge to the teaching and understanding of 'true' history provided by this book.

In the case of evolution and creationism, it will probably be a long time before the issues are untangled sufficiently from their fictitious representation to move forward with genuine education on the matter. In the meantime, however, *Summer for the Gods* reminds us to maintain a suitable level of skepticism in all science-religion discussion. The slate is far from clean.

ENDNOTES

1   Daniel C. Dennett, *Darwin's Dangerous Idea: Evolution and the Meanings of Life*, Penguin, Harmondsworth, 1995, p. 516.

2   Quoted in Carol Iannone, 'The truth about Inherit the Wind', *First Things*, 1997, *70*, pp. 28-33. It hardly needs pointing out that Bryant was quite right; the economic rationalism we see around us today is the working-out in society of a Darwinistic view of business.

3   5th October, 1997.

4   *84 (4)*, March 1998, pp. 1553-1554.

Other books from Matthias Media...

The Essence of Darwinism

Is Darwinism true? Is it the only theory that can explain our origins? Should we care? Are we taking Genesis seriously enough?

In her fourth book in *The Essence of* series, Dr Kirsten Birkett considers these frequently asked questions. In an area in which there seem to be so many conflicting answers, she takes a fresh look at the controversy by getting behind the surface disputes to look at what is really being argued over. At the same time, this book provides a compact and accessible summary of the important points of the Darwinian theory so far.

The Essence of Darwinism is an easy-to-read book for all thinkers from senior high school onwards.

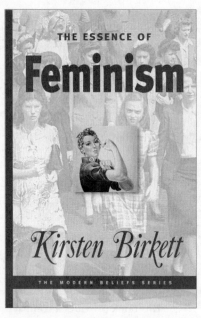